Org Design for Design Orgs

Building and Managing In-House Design Teams

Peter Merholz and Kristin Skinner

Beijing · Boston · Farnham · Sebastopol · Tokyo

Org Design for Design Orgs
by Peter Merholz and Kristin Skinner

Published by O'Reilly Media, Inc., 1005 Gravenstein Highway North, Sebastopol, CA 95472.

O'Reilly books may be purchased for educational, business, or sales promotional use. Online editions are also available for most titles (*safaribooksonline.com*). For more information, contact our corporate/institutional sales department: (800) 998-9938 or *corporate@oreilly.com*.

Acquisitions Editor: Nick Lombardi
Developmental Editor: Angela Rufino
Production Editor: Melanie Yarbrough
Copyeditor: Jasmine Kwityn
Proofreader: Rachel Monaghan

Indexer: Lucie Haskins
Cover Designer: Randy Comer
Interior Designers: Ron Bilodeau and Monica Kamsvaag
Illustrator: Rebecca Demarest
Compositor: Melanie Yarbrough

September 2016: First Edition.

Revision History for the First Edition:

2016-08-11   First release

See *http://oreilly.com/catalog/errata.csp?isbn=0636920044949* for release details.

978-1-491-93840-9

[LSI]

[*contents*]

[*Foreword*]

"The space between is just as important as the objects themselves."

MY 10TH-GRADE GRAPHIC ARTS teacher had just finished tearing into my layout, complaining that my kerning was off, my margins were wrong, and my proportions were uneven. I was manually laying a page of text and images, and having just burned my hand on the waxer, I wasn't interested in his advice. What did it matter if the top was off by a millimeter? There's plenty of room on the page for the rest of the...

Oh.

It turns out Mr. Mackie was less concerned about my ability to follow his instructions precisely and more interested in my understanding of the relationships between the content on the page—the letters, the images, the whitespace. Without planning and proper attention, the effects can ripple through the work. I didn't need to work on my kerning—I needed to get better at seeing the bigger picture.

This lesson stood out more than any other and has followed me throughout my design career. There is a distinct rhythm to content on a page, objects on a screen, and people in physical space. The sum of these interactions defines the success or failure of the design. As designers, we're charged with solving detailed problems, and those solutions are often most powerful when balanced with a larger perspective.

I've often thought about design teams in terms of organization and operation—the structure and methods created to help designers do their best work. Designers who have worked both at an agency and in-house have probably experienced a few different approaches to creative problem solving. We've seen the tension between speed, cost, and quality. We've felt the desire to get design a seat at the table. And we've experienced the fear and opportunity once we've sat down.

The reality is that designers have never been in a better situation to make an impact on the world. Our methods and thinking are valued and respected. We not only make the things but we help create the strategy that brings the things to life. So now what?

We get better.

We get better at understanding business, the needs of people, the operations of our creativity, and the framework in which we find the freedom to apply our skills. We get better at being active partners to analysts, marketers, and engineers. We get better at building services and experiences, not just features. We get better at seeing the bigger picture.

This book finds itself in the right spot at the right time. It doesn't take a place next to the piles of books attempting to define what is UX and what is UI. It serves to help create a framework for design teams to thrive. Peter and Kristin have spent years working with many designers, agencies, organizations, and companies, and have seen what works and what could work better. With the increasing growth of in-house design teams, design leaders need the right tools to build successful organizations. This book gives insight into methods for growth and support of design teams that are rarely discussed. It shines light in the spaces between problems, projects, and people.

We're witnessing an amazing maturity in our craft. As we expand our opportunity for impact, we must get better at creating frameworks to support those efforts. This text is your start.

ANDREW CROW,
HEAD OF DESIGN AT MEDIUM

[*Preface*]

Why We Wrote This Book

DESIGN BOOKS TYPICALLY DISCUSS design practice—tools, processes, and methods for doing design work, and case studies that show how that work has been applied to real-world problems. These books are meant for design practitioners who are looking to improve their craft.

This is not that kind of design book. Instead, this book responds to a profound shift that has occurred within enterprises over the past 10 years. Businesses and other organizations have realized that design, like sales, marketing, and information technology, must now be a core competency. Design has proven vital to business success, whether reducing costs and customer churn, or increasing revenue through creation of new value. This has driven companies to seriously invest in internal design capabilities.

The thing is, design is way less mature than other corporate functions, and its practice and impact suffer because of its lack of sophistication. Companies aren't realizing the potential of their design investments. Most business leaders are not designers, and so don't know how best to establish design in their organizations. Many design leaders, with backgrounds in the practice of their craft, don't understand managerial and operational issues, and struggle with the organizational aspects of building and leading teams.

Org Design for Design Orgs is for those business and design leaders. This is the book we wish we had as we began our careers building and managing design teams. Like so many others, we figured it out as we went along, stumbling toward a set of approaches that work pretty well. We share what we've learned not because we have it all figured out (far from it!), but because it's time to elevate the dialogue around design operations and management.

This is a handbook for making the most out of design organizations within enterprises, regardless of their present size and sophistication. Instead of design practice methods and tools, it features maturity models, organizational frameworks, guides for staffing and retaining talent, and recommendations for successful cross-team collaboration.

The Authors

Peter Merholz's career in design management began during the first web boom at Internet startup Epinions, where he built a small team and realized that the best thing he could do was get out of their way. He followed this with establishing Adaptive Path, a world-renowned user experience consultancy. In helping it grow from the original 7 to nearly 50, Peter led much of the recruiting and hiring, scoped and led dozens of projects and programs, and codified the key roles and responsibilities of project teams. After leaving Adaptive Path, Peter tackled a series of in-house challenges, most notably as VP of Global Design at Groupon. There, he took a team of nearly 30 product and communication designers in three different locations, and grew it to nearly 60 in six locations, while improving their effectiveness and shifting design from an afterthought to a critical function.

Kristin Skinner began her career in design management by working at a slew of Bay Area startups in various design capacities, and then took a Design Program Manager role at Microsoft at a time when there were just 400 designers at a company of 90,000. After an initial stint in the Server and Tools division, she switched to a Design Manager role focused on user experience strategy, and device and services design at Microsoft's Pioneer Studios, which was created to incubate new business opportunities for emerging consumer experiences in gaming, entertainment, and media. She managed the end-to-end work of a team of 25 UX, visual, and motion designers focused on strategy, vision, prototyping, and design for mobile.

After four years at Microsoft, she joined Adaptive Path, where she spearheaded its program management efforts, streamlined operations, co-programmed and co-hosted its annual Managing Experience conference, and shaped and led over 50 projects and programs. After Capital One's acquisition of Adaptive Path, she remained, focusing on transitioning the consultancy to an in-house specialty design team while establishing and leading a new Design Management practice across the entire design organization with a team of 15 design managers (and growing!).

How This Book Is Structured

Org Design for Design Orgs contains four thematic parts:

Part I

Because design is a squishy term that means different things to different people, the book begins by grounding the reader with a set of core concepts and definition of design. Chapter 1 explains the forces behind design's ascension within business. Chapter 2 redefines "design" with a far greater purview than it is typically given, and discusses the organizational implications when design is granted that expansiveness.

Part II

This part is made up of just Chapter 3, which outlines the 12 qualities of effective design organizations. This chapter stands on its own as an overview of the many concerns that must be addressed, serving as a kind of maturity model against which any design organization can be assessed. If you only have time to read one chapter, make it this one.

Part III

The next two chapters tackle matters of organizational structure and evolution. In Chapter 4, we discuss centralized and decentralized approaches, and propose a hybrid model that enables the best of both worlds. With that as a foundation, in Chapter 5 we share our thoughts on the roles that make up a modern design organization, and how a design team evolves over time, from the initial 2 members to 60 and beyond.

Part IV

The remaining chapters focus on the brass tacks of running a design organization. Chapter 6 provides step-by-step detail of establishing headcount, sourcing candidates, and navigating the interview process. Once on the team, employees need to know how they can grow. Chapter 7 outlines a flexible skills-building and levels framework for designers, supporting a myriad of career paths. Key to the success of a design organization is a strong sense of identity, and Chapter 8 shows how a team's values, environments, and activities lead to making it a great place to work. With a solid culture established, designers are better suited to collaborate cross-functionally, the subject of Chapter 9.

Acknowledgments

Both authors wish to thank Mary Treseler for bringing us onboard at O'Reilly, and Angela Rufino and Nick Lombardi for sticking with us throughout. Our writing benefited from the many conversations we had with design and business leaders: Chris Avore, Bob Baxley, Sara Beckman, Leah Buley, Dave Cronin, Catherine Courage, Mike Davidson, Kaaren Hanson, Sabine Junginger, Braden Kowitz, Chris McCarthy, Lesley Mottla, Kai En Ong, Margaret Stewart, Milissa Tarquini, and Secil Watson. And we are grateful to early readers and reviewers Ellen Beldner, Andrew Crow, Adam Cutler, Erik Flowers, and Lori Kaplan.

PETER

This journey would have never taken place without my coauthor Kristin, and I'm grateful for our chance to once again work together.

In addition to the people mentioned above, I want to thank those with whom I had less formal, but still informative conversations, including Richard Dalton, Priyanka Kakar, Jared Spool, Russ Unger, and Todd Wilkens.

And I'm most grateful for the support of my wife Stacy Kozakavich, and our children Jules and Dorothy, who still don't really know exactly what I do.

KRISTIN

As design practitioners, we can design experiences, organizations, communities, our lives. And as design managers, we naturally focus on others—our teams, customers, and the participants in the design and delivery of the experience. As we design not just screens, flows, processes, and services, but focus across fields to design systems, beliefs, and organizations that make up great experiences, we recognize that we rarely go it alone. We become obsessed with what works for the customer and how to prove it; we measure feedback and learn from it while optimizing for both speed and scale. And we are driven to get the most out of our teams by focusing them on their best skills, connecting the right efforts for impact, and ensuring value of the experience and efficiencies in the work. This book is meant to be a playbook to help guide that journey.

In late spring 2015, Peter and I were having an informal chat about design organizations. Having similar but complementary experiences, we half-joked "we should write a book!" which soon turned into an outline, which turned into a proposal, which turned into *Org Design for Design Orgs* some 15 months later. We approached the process in the best way we knew how—draft an outline, make a plan, identify and talk to experts, incorporate feedback, adjust the plan, refine the outline, create some talks, have more conversations, incorporate more feedback, teach some workshops, adjust the plan again, and actually write the thing. Exceptional support, willingness to share, and thoughtful discussions by everyone Peter mentioned (and deadlines!) helped bring us to this point.

Thanks to Peter for his perspective and energy; thanks also to my colleagues over the past six years at Adaptive Path for their wealth of knowledge, especially Brandon Schauer for the guidance, support, and clearing of pathways when needed, and Scott Zimmer for recognizing the value and potential of the field of design management applied at scale to a financial services organization, and for giving me the opportunity and latitude to establish and lead this discipline.

Thanks to my Design Management team and their wealth of perspectives, contributions, support, and encouragement. I'm honored to be surrounded by such a motivated, passionate, and dedicated group of GSD (get shit done) experts.

Finally, I'm thankful for my family and my daily inspiration, my boy, Vaughn KS Miller, who unwittingly and effortlessly reminds me that I have much to learn from his perspective—you motivate me, teach me patience, and make me laugh every single day, and for that, I am grateful beyond words.

[1]

Why Design? Why Now?

As with much of the economy, September 2009 was an uncertain time for the technology sector. The markets were mostly recovered after the global financial collapse, but it wasn't clear if this would sustain or if a double-dip recession would undo the recovery. That month, a corporate acquisition occurred that has ripple effects to this day, though not in any way predicted at the time. Intuit, the leading provider for personal and small business financial management software, paid $170 million to acquire Mint, a service that aggregated all your financial accounts into a single dashboard. Mint had been operating for only 2 years, had 35 employees, and had about 1.5 million users. Revenues supposedly had grown fast, but were never shared.

Most surprising, Mint didn't own the core aggregation technology— that came from Yodlee. Mint's innovation was a smooth and delightful user experience on top of that technology, which in turn created a passionate, active, and growing user base. In large part, Mint was acquired for its design, as that was the primary factor contributing to its desirable metrics. This proved to be a lightbulb moment in Silicon Valley, along with the rise of Apple at the time. Mergers and acquisitions activity for design firms and designer-led companies accelerated after 2010,[1] and every startup and tech company realized they needed a design competency in order to stay competitive.

Silicon Valley is such an idiosyncratic business environment, it would be easy for companies outside its bubble to dismiss this embrace of design. However, it's not just next-generation tech companies that are increasing this investment. In 2012, two tech stalwarts made big moves, with GE establishing a UX Center of Excellence, and IBM announcing

---

1 As shown in KPCB's *#Design In Tech Report 2016* (*http://www.kpcb.com/blog/design-in-tech-report-2016*).

plans to hire 1,000 designers over the span of 5 years. Then banks Capital One and BBVA each acquired design firms. In management consulting, Accenture acquired Fjord, and McKinsey acquired Lunar. What's going on here? By addressing this question, we can establish a framework for thinking about the impact design can have on an organization.

"The Power of Design"

As companies and their offerings get more complicated, old ways of management have successfully run their course. In the 20th century, business was dominated by "scientific management" (aka "Taylorism") wherein workers' activities were minutely analyzed, new practices were specified in exacting and mind-numbing detail, and independent thought on the part of laborers was discouraged, as the solution had been figured out by management.[2] With the growing capabilities of computation, the mantra of the 80s and 90s was Business Process Reengineering and Six Sigma. These were methodologies for removing waste from development and production processes, streamlining supply chains, and generally making companies more efficient. These tools worked beautifully, helping companies increase their bottom lines by reining in needless costs. Dell became the market leader for personal computers because it was better than any other company at managing a supply chain.

However, systems have limits to their efficiency. Beyond a certain point, additional streamlining efforts return negligible gains. Once a company realizes it has run out of optimizations, the only way to grow is through increasing the top line. This led to the cult of "innovation" that began in the late 1990s and continues to this day.

At first, the innovation conversation turned to science and technology as the key wellsprings of creativity. Around 2004, the conversation broadened, as indicated by *BusinessWeek* placing the design firm IDEO on its cover, touting "The Power of Design" (Figure 1-1). The empathetic, inventive, and iterative aspects of design practice were seen as new ways to help business break out of its overly analytical rut.

---

2   To better understand the 20th century's mania for efficiency, Wikipedia's entry on Scientific Management (*https://en.wikipedia.org/wiki/Scientific_management*) is a great place to start.

FIGURE 1-1

Cover of *BusinessWeek*, May 17, 2004

"Software Is Eating the World"

Parallel to this quest for innovation, another realization slowly dawned. As Marc Andreessen put it in his 2011 seminal essay for the *Wall Street Journal*: "Software is eating the world." For decades, software was a product, something software companies like Microsoft or Oracle or Adobe produced. But then, with the rise of the Internet, a fundamental shift happened. Companies realized that, regardless of their business, software was core to their infrastructure. Every company is becoming, to some degree, a software company. A company might have been thought of as an "airline," "hotel," "manufacturer," "bank," "consulting firm," and so on, but over time a greater and greater part of their business was dedicated to creating software to support and enable their operations. For example, GE, which until recently thought of itself as an industrial manufacturer, realized it was also the world's 14th largest software company—the software to power all of these big machines.

Software, by its nature, dwells in abstractions, and making sense of those abstractions proves difficult for most people. Recognizing this, software is one field with relatively decent investment in design, under the guise of "human–computer interaction," "interaction design," "interface design," or even "usability." As design is seen as a best practice in software development, and more companies invest more in their software capabilities, it follows that more companies begin investing more in design.

The Consumerization of All Software

Not only is there more software being created, there's also a growing requirement that the software be good. "Good" is a squishy term, but in this context it means it's no longer sufficient for software to simply "check off all the features." Feature parity was an acceptable strategy when software was a less mature discipline, but now software competes not just on function, but experience as well. As software users work with more software tools, they become sophisticated, learning to appreciate software that works well, and denigrate software that doesn't.

For a while this affected only consumer products, where individuals had the power to choose what to buy. Enterprise software design remained terrible for a few reasons: the person buying the software was usually not the person using it; the people using it had no alternative; a belief that bad design could be overcome through training;

and a sense that work shouldn't be fun or pleasant, and that software should reflect such seriousness. However, the market for enterprise software has evolved. Companies realized the productivity drag of poor software, and users, as their sophistication grew, were less willing to put up with bad design. Enterprise software companies found themselves losing customers because of their poor design. This "consumerization of IT" has accelerated as people who have been steeped in digital technology since childhood (read: "millennials") have entered the workforce, and they have higher expectations from technology than those who preceded them. This means some of the biggest investments in design are happening on the enterprise side, such as IBM's plan to hire 1,000 designers, nearly all dedicated to enterprise software.

Everything-as-a-Service

Traditional software could be thought of as a product—when it was finished, it was shipped, put in boxes sold on shelves, or directly installed on machines. In a networked world, software is never finished, and is continually optimized, enhanced, and deployed. This shift has been so fundamental that software companies associated with boxes on shelves, like Microsoft and Adobe, now generate revenue through subscription models, where customers don't own the software, but license access to it.

The always-on, networked, and continually modified nature of software has altered the dynamic between seller and buyer. It is now a continual relationship, and accordingly, every company is becoming not only a software company but also a services firm.

Apple is still seen as primarily a hardware products firm, but much of its success is due to intelligent incorporation of services, starting with the Apple Stores in 2001 (inspired by the white glove service received at top hotels like the Four Seasons[3]) and continuing with the iTunes Music Store (which enhanced the experience of iPod, and also allowed Apple to place the iTunes Trojan Horse on millions of computers), the iOS and OS X App Stores, and most recently Apple Music. With the Internet of Things, whole categories of consumer electronics (e.g.,

---

3   Jerry Useem, "Apple: America's Best Retailer," *Forbes*, March 8, 2007, (*http://archive. fortune.com/magazines/fortune/fortune_archive/2007/03/19/8402321/index.htm*).

pedometers [Figure 1-2], thermostats, smoke detectors, security cameras, refrigerators, televisions) become Internet-enabled. With their data in the cloud accessible from everywhere, these products have evolved into always-on services.[4]

FIGURE 1-2
The fitness tracker Jawbone UP3 has no display. The device has no value without its app, a cloud-based service storing the user's data and providing personalized insights. The physical product is simply a part of a larger service ecosystem. (Photograph by Peter Merholz)

If the company was not a services firm already, this requires a fundamental shift in how a company thinks of and interacts with its customers. In a product world, where people purchased goods through an intermediary (i.e., retailer) and there was no connectivity, companies had only a vague sense of who their customers were, and only if their customers did things like fill out registration cards. Now, to use

4 Mike Kuniavsky's notion of "service avatars," explored in his book *Smart Things* (Morgan Kaufmann, 2010), addresses this shift in detail.

these products, customers create accounts, and the service tracks their behavior in detail. Companies have a responsibility to better know and serve these customers on an ongoing basis.

Double-Edged Sword of User Empowerment

However, it's not just about "becoming a service." Even if you were already a services firm, the underlying technology, the very reason that every company can now be a service, enables a new reality about delivering services: it is more complicated than ever.

Before the mid-1990s, if you wanted to interact with a company, you did so in person, by phone, by fax, or through postal mail. Since then, there's been an explosion of digital touchpoints: initially the Web and email, and then online chat, social media, and mobile apps.

Networked software not only meant new ways to communicate—it also provided new means for customers to act. Pre-Internet, if a services firm like a bank used software, it was primarily as an internal tool used by a trained professional. Anything customer-facing, such as the software in ATMs and telephone banking, was limited to basic functions. The desktop Web then allowed businesses to avail customers of the power of these formerly internal systems.

Customers were willing to adopt these complicated tools because they appreciated having greater direct control. Companies encouraged this because it helped reduce labor costs. However, internal users could be expected to be using such tools for hours a day, whereas external users were more likely to use them for minutes a week or even a month. Creating something understandable to a non-expert for such relatively little use required deep rethinking. And as competitors achieved feature parity, customers chose services not just because of the capabilities provided, but also the quality of the user experience. This led traditional service industries (finance, retail, travel, hospitality) to closely follow consumer tech companies (such as Apple, Yahoo, and Netscape) to be among the first to build significant in-house design organizations.

The dichotomy between complexity and simplicity is exacerbated by the rise of mobile phones. By providing a new point of access, their very existence increases complexity. However, design for mobile needs to be more streamlined and straightforward to fit within its constraints— smaller screens, slower processors, and less precise pointing devices.

Design Can Be So Much More Than "Problem Solving"

Business in the industrial and information ages of the 19th and 20th centuries was dominated by the analytical approaches typical in scientific management and engineering. Such reductive approaches are insufficient for tackling the complex challenges companies now face. This has led to greater investment in design for the following reasons:

- Squeezing greater efficiency has run its course, and design's generative qualities are seen as a means to realize new business value.

- Given software's abstract nature, design is required to tether the experience to something people can understand; with networked software, this challenge is exponentialized.

- The shift from products to services, with umpteen touchpoints by which someone chooses to interact, places greater reliance on design for coordination so as not to overwhelm the customer.

These challenges explain corporations' willingness to spend on design, but if we focus only on known problems, we limit the potential impact that design can have on a company. While design is often associated with problem solving, the irony is that this view represents the same reductionist mindset that created the challenges that design is being brought in to address.

Problem solving is only the tip of the iceberg for design. Beneath the surface, design is a powerful tool for problem framing, ensuring that what is being addressed is worth tackling. Go deeper still, and you discover that the core opportunity for design is to inject humanism into work. The best designed products and services don't simply solve problems—they connect deeply with people. When design is combined with social sciences like anthropology and sociology, and other creative disciplines such as writing, there exists the possibility of creating a powerful expression of the human experience. As Steve Jobs said:

> Design is the fundamental soul of a man-made creation that ends up expressing itself in successive outer layers of the product or service.[5]

---

5   Steve Jobs, "Apple's One-Dollar-a-Year Man," *Fortune*, January 24, 2000, (*http://archive. fortune.com/magazines/fortune/fortune_archive/2000/01/24/272277/index.htm*).

[2]

Realizing the Potential of Design

COMPANIES INVEST IN DESIGN in order to manage the software-driven complexity of their businesses. There's a sense that design makes things "better," by making them more attractive, more desirable, and easier to use. However, many, and probably most, of the people responsible for bringing design into their organizations have only a rudimentary understanding of what it can deliver. They perceive design primarily as aesthetics, styling, and appearances.

We ended the last chapter with a Steve Jobs quote about design, so let's begin this one with perhaps his most famous statement on the matter:

> Most people make the mistake of thinking design is what it looks like. People think it's this veneer—that the designers are handed this box and told, "Make it look good!" That's not what we think design is. It's not just what it looks like and feels like. Design is how it works.[1]

Jobs' definition is inspiring, but hard to make actionable. For our purposes, we prefer the definition from noted user experience expert Jared Spool, who wrote, "Design is the rendering of intent." He continues, "The designer imagines an outcome and puts forth activities to make that outcome real."[2] This might seem vague or abstract, but that's purposeful—it points out that "design" is happening all the time, in a variety of contexts, whether or not we think of it as that. For a company to better deliver on its own intentions, it benefits from incorporating mindful design throughout its activities.

---

1 Rob Walker, "The Guts of a New Machine", *The New York Times,* November 30, 2003, (*http://www.nytimes.com/2003/11/30/magazine/30IPOD.html*).

2 Jared M. Spool, "Design Is the Rendering of Intent," User Interface Engeineering (UIE), December 30, 2013, (*http://www.uie.com/articles/design_rendering_intent/*).

Rob Brunner, founder of product design consultancy Ammunition (best known for their work on Beats by Dre), gave a presentation at the 2016 O'Reilly Design Conference titled "Design Is a Process, Not an Event,"[3] where he shared what he saw in the evolution of design. He points out that until recently, design was seen as a step in a chain (Figure 2-1).

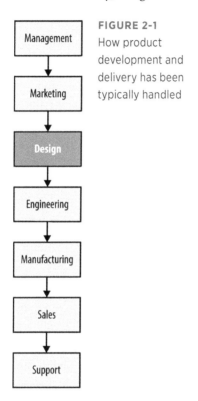

FIGURE 2-1
How product development and delivery has been typically handled

He contends that what is now becoming clear is that design is not a standalone event, but a process that works best when infused throughout a product development lifecycle (Figure 2-2).

---

3 Robert Brunner, "Design Is a Process, Not an Event," 2016 O'Reilly Design Conference, January 21, 2016, (*https://www.youtube.com/watch?v=hx8NjTo9Phc*).

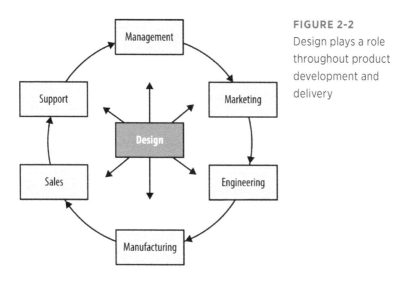

FIGURE 2-2
Design plays a role throughout product development and delivery

All Design Is Service Design

As every company becomes a services firm, it follows that the opportunity for design is to make every part of that service experience more intentional. An emerging discipline called "service design" reframes how organizations utilize design. Historically, design has been focused on the creation of things, whether in service of marketing (advertising, branding, packaging) or product (industrial design, software design). Service design applies many of the same practices, but pulls back from this emphasis on artifacts, instead assuming a broader view in an effort to understand the relationships between people (customers, frontline employees, management, partners) and the activities they take part in. Artifacts are no longer considered on their own, but as tools in a larger service ecosystem.

At the heart of service design is the customer journey. Mapping these journeys begins before the customer even knows about a company, traces the customer's interactions with the company across different touchpoints, and ends when that customer moves on from the relationship. This mapping provides an alternative perspective on service delivery from how organizations are typically structured. It reveals that a customer interacts with marketing, sales, product, and support in a manner that's typically impeded by departmental silos. It also highlights how certain touchpoints get overloaded with poorly aligned interactions. For example, a company might use email:

- To deliver marketing and promotions

- To extend certain product experiences (daily updates, results of saved searches, etc.)

- For technical or customer support communications

If these messages are not coordinated well, the customer is overrun by email, and may choose to simply ignore that channel altogether, thus inadvertently inhibiting the company's ability to communicate.

This has implications for organizational structure. For example, many companies have separate marketing and product design teams. However, to a customer, marketing and product are simply points along the same journey, often delivered in the same media—web browser, mobile app, and email—and would benefit from coherence in the team that designs them. The logical conclusion of the journey mindset is that design practices that are currently kept separate—marketing, communication, environments, and digital products—all contribute to a single journey, and ought to be coordinated. Additionally, this mindset shows how design can support things that it typically is not involved with, such as sales and customer support.

This book is not a how-to on service design. For that, we recommend Marc Stickdorn, Markus Edgar Hormess, Adam Lawrence, and Jakob Schneider's *This Is Service Design Doing* (O'Reilly, 2016) and Andy Polaine, Ben Reason, and Lavrans Løvlie's *Service Design: From Insight to Implementation* (Rosenfeld Media, 2013). Our point is to recognize that contributions from design shouldn't be limited to marketing and product efforts, but instead infused throughout the entire service. Wherever the customer and your organization interact, that touchpoint will be improved by design's intentionality, and this has implications on the shape of the design team.

The Double Diamond

To frame design's ability to contribute broadly, we use the Double Diamond (Figure 2-3), a diagrammatic model of product definition and delivery.

It's a bit of a simplification, and shouldn't be construed as a strict process. Still, it serves to depict how designers best approach and solve problems. The first diamond, Definition, addresses the steps needed to articulate a strategy and develop a plan for your offering. The second diamond, Execution, is about implementing that plan.

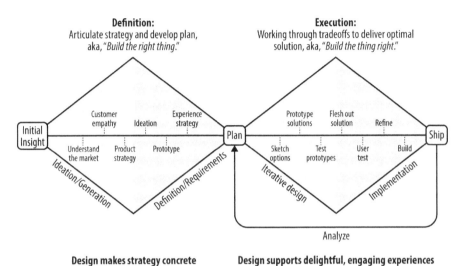

Too often, project teams settle for linear thinking, where the team leader (typically a product or marketing manager) puts forth an idea that is then taken as the solution, and teams just march toward its implementation. The genius of the diamond shape is that it shows, for both definition and execution, that the team first engages in divergent thinking that broadens the possibility space, before turning a corner and practicing the convergent thinking that narrows in on a specific solution.

DESIGN DEFINES

In most organizations, designers are not engaged until the second diamond, when strategic and planning decisions have already been made, and their role is to execute on a set of requirements or a creative brief. While service design encourages a broader role throughout the entire customer experience, it may still remain quite superficial and execution oriented. If organizations are going to embrace all that design has to offer, this must involve influencing product and even corporate strategy.

Since at least the advent of scientific management, the predominant mode of business strategy has been analytical. Reduce processes and practices to their elemental components, and squeeze the most out of them. Even product marketing, which should be rooted in creativity and user experience, instead relies on practices such as market segmentation and sizing, surveys to assess consumer sentiment and satisfaction, and product requirements that focus on Cost of Goods Sold (COGS) and the Four Ps (Product, Price, Promotion, and Place).

This stereotypically "left-brained" approach has served business well for quite a while, but has run aground of the connected services economy. Services are predicated on relationships with and between people, a human messiness that these analytical means insufficiently address. What's called for are more "right-brained" approaches that are holistic instead of analytical, and that are generative instead of reductive. And key to successful human relationships is empathy, a quality distinctly lacking in traditional business practice. Good design practice is an expression of deep empathy, and businesses are realizing that bringing design into the definition conversation (the first diamond) provides better balance in their thinking. At Airbnb, extensive user research was done to build deep personas for Hosts and Guests, which included their respective customer journeys. Airbnb then brought on an artist from Pixar to illustrate key moments in the journey, and these visual storyboards help orient design, engineering, and business around common goals.

DESIGN MAKES STRATEGY CONCRETE

When strategy focuses on optimization, directives can be written as a set of metrics, such as improving conversion rates or increasing engagement. When it's about delivering products to market segments, directives are a list of features and the audiences they serve. But when it's about creating new offerings in an uncertain market context, these reductive approaches fall short. If you remain in the abstraction of spreadsheet formulas or bullet-pointed requirements on PowerPoint decks, four issues arise:

- There are trade-offs or conflicts within the requirements that are not apparent (say, improving ease of use or task completion, while also empowering users with more functionality), and so a chosen strategy might actually be unworkable.

- Each stakeholder has their own, unstated understanding of what that strategy means, and their misalignment is not evident until the building process, which proves too late for resolving the conflict.

- What's being developed doesn't accord with the vision stakeholders had in their heads.

- Internal teams are not motivated by abstractions, and may deliver tepid work that satisfies the requirements, but goes no further.

An architect would never propose a building design without presenting stakeholders a scale model; filmmakers write scripts and draw storyboards before rounding up a crew and committing to a foot of film. Likewise, bringing the design activities of user research, sketching, ideation, and rapid prototyping into strategy work ensures these issues won't arise. Low-fidelity sketches quickly make apparent shortcomings in an incoherent or incomplete strategy. Even if the strategy is solid, by making it concrete, you ensure that all stakeholders have a shared understanding of the implications of that strategy. If there are issues with the strategy, they get addressed in this early stage, when iteration is cheap, and not during development, when making changes can be quite costly. And by embodying the strategy in a clear vision, project teams have a compelling, motivating goal to attain, a "north star" that encourages them to deliver better than they've ever delivered before.

But design shouldn't be limited to just embodying a strategy established by the business. Design practices should actively contribute to and shape the strategy. Because sketching and ideation are relatively inexpensive, design employs divergent thinking to explore a range of options, feeling them out, or even putting them in front of customers to gauge acceptance. In this way, design brings forth solutions that had not yet even been considered, and does so in a way that can garner meaningful external feedback.

Even with all these obvious benefits, many organizations resist making strategy concrete. By remaining in abstraction as long as possible, hard decisions do not have to be made. Trade-offs do not have to be realized, and everyone can believe that their pet idea will see it through. When design contributes to strategy, it challenges this mindset, and forces stakeholders to commit.

CUSTOMER-CENTERED PLANNING

In between the two diamonds exists the project plan. The plan typically contains two parts: (a) a vision for where the product is ultimately headed (informed by the strategy work), and (b) a series of steps to realize that vision, sometimes called a roadmap or backlog.

It might seem like a small thing, but how that plan is shaped can be crucial for the offering's overall success. These plans are typically organized by importance to the business and estimated effort. Features are scored across these two criteria, and then ranked. And then the teams plow through the list.

The shortcoming of this approach is illustrated in the diagram in Figure 2-4, drawn by agile coach Henrik Kniberg:[4]

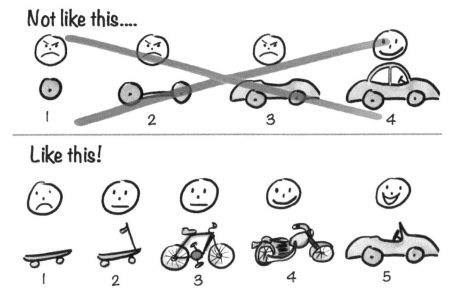

Henrik Kniberg

FIGURE 2-4

Henrik Kniberg's drawing of a preferred product development approach

---

4 Henrik explains the diagram in detail here:in the blog post "Making Sense of MVP (Minimum Viable Product)—and Why I Prefer Earliest Testable/Usable/Lovable" (*http://blog.crisp.se/2016/01/25/henrikkniberg/making-sense-of-mvp*).

When releasing products or services in an iterative and accretive fashion, it's important to keep in mind the customer's experience every step of the way. So, even though the first row gets to the ultimate release faster, taking four steps, it does so by sacrificing user happiness at each earlier release. This means, in practicality, users won't stick around for that ultimate release. They will have moved on to other options.

While it takes five steps to get to the ultimate release in the second row, at every stage there's a holistic experience. The initial experience might not be what the customer wants, but as the organization learns through successive releases, they deliver more happiness sooner. Also, through that learning, the organization can correct course, and realize a different ultimate delivery ("the convertible") that serves their customers even better than their original vision ("the sedan"). Design's role in this process is to bring an empathetic perspective that understands what customers will find desirable, and influence the roadmap to reflect that.

THE BULK OF DESIGN IS EXECUTION

We've dwelled on strategic and planning matters because these are not widely appreciated, and are essential for design to deliver to its fullest extent. That said, the bulk of an organization's design effort (80%–90%) will be within that second diamond of execution. A shortcoming of the Double Diamond diagram is that it suggests that for every act of definition, there is an act of execution. In fact, after the creation of a plan, execution occurs iteratively, knocking down elements of the roadmap with each pass (Figure 2-5).

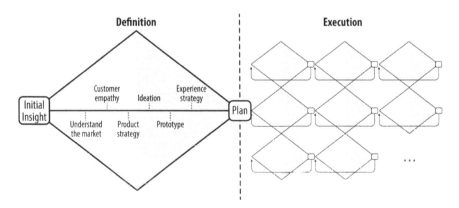

FIGURE 2-5
Definition occurs once in a while, and execution occurs iteratively against the established plan

The specific design practices shift when going from definition to execution. When informing strategy, design is more generalized, drawing on user research, sketching, and prototyping. A sketch might represent a software interface, a piece of marketing collateral, or a physical object. Execution brings with it a focus on specific design disciplines. Designing for software, designing for marketing and communications, and designing for physical products are quite distinct practices, and require specialists well-versed in those media.

Bringing Design In-House

The history of business and design is typically one of clients and design firms. Bell Laboratories and Henry Dreyfuss, IBM with Eliot Noyes, Paul Rand and the Eames Studio, Apple and Frogdesign. Design was an outsourced specialty, needed in a tightly defined fashion, usually for logos and products.

At the rise of the Web, most companies handled the need for design through external vendors. They didn't have capabilities in-house, and weren't sure it was worth the investment. Twenty years in, it's clear that we are in a new normal. The shift to networked software and multi-touchpoint services has created a fundamentally chaotic and unpredictable environment that requires continuous delivery.

Design can no longer be a specification that is handed off, built, and never seen again. It needs to be embedded within the strategy and development processes, and its practitioners must be deeply familiar with the company's mission, vision, and practices. To make this work with an outsourced partner is possible, but very expensive, and raises concerns about an external firm's alignment with the company's values and ideals. It's simply more straightforward to build in-house design competencies that are organizationally and operationally conjoined with functions such as marketing, engineering, and support.

The Three-Legged Stool

This continuous delivery requires changes within product teams. Historically, the ultimate authority in product development lived with someone representing "the business," such as product marketing, general managers, or product managers, who took in an understanding of market needs, articulated a set of requirements, and gave that to teams to build. For software products, the technology became too complex to locate all decisions in a single product manager—delivering quality work required that people with technical depth also be given authority. This led to teams with joint product and engineering leadership. As we enter a world of connected software and services, the primacy of relationships and need for quality user experience cannot be addressed only through technical and business expertise. Designers should no longer be handed briefs and requirements, but instead be part of the conversation earlier to make sure that their empathetic perspective is represented. The reality of contemporary product and service delivery is a messy one, and requires the productive tension between business, technology, and design. Think of them as the three legs that the offering rests upon (Figure 2-6). If any leg is deficient, what is delivered will be wobbly.

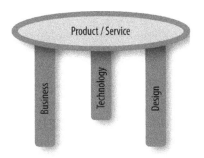

FIGURE 2-6

The three-legged stool of product and service development and delivery

THE EXPANDED ROLE OF DESIGN

Pulling all this together, we arrive at an expanded role for design. For decades, the typical operating mode for design was to receive a brief or requirements from "the business," limited to the look and feel of the product or the brand impact of a marketing campaign, and execute on that.

The rise of software led to more complex products, and a subsequent realization that many requirements didn't make sense when users tried to actually operate the system—a lack of empathy led to confusing experiences. Designers created the discipline of user experience to compensate for this shortcoming, developing a set of methods (user research, usability testing, personas, workflows, wireframes) and fostering a user-centered mindset that helped manage this complexity and make it understandable to people.

It then became clear that these practices are useful not just in the execution of a product. As companies improved instrumentation of their experiences, they realized that such approaches drive real business value. They can be used to meaningfully contribute to a service's definition, and designers found themselves part of the strategic conversations about what should be built. Design had earned its long-sought-after "seat at the table."

And from that vantage point, it has become clear that the frontier for design is to play a role not only in every stage of development from idea to final offering, but to be woven into every aspect of the service experience from marketing to product to support. The challenge is that most organizations are structured and run in a way that inhibits this potential. In subsequent chapters, we'll show how to establish, organize, and evolve a design team that can realize this expanded mandate.

Design and "User Experience"

It is common, when discussing design as we have, to also refer to "user experience." In fact, many would call the kind of software design we're discussing "user experience design." We have two reasons we're avoiding this specific association between design and user experience.

The first reason is that when you try to find or articulate a definition of "user experience design," things get muddier, not clearer. Most of the time, people interpret "user experience design" to mean "interaction design with some information architecture," and focus on the creation of workflows and wireframes. Some of the time, though, UX design is expected to include user research and strategy, and other times it's associated with visual interface design. Throughout this book, we avoid "user experience design" in favor of referring to specific disciplines.

The second reason is that automatically lumping design with user experience gives short shrift to all the other disciplines that contribute to the user experience. A user's experience is the emergent outcome of numerous contributions, including design, but also engineering (technical performance has a huge impact on user experience), marketing (how expectations are managed affects the user experience), and customer care (a bad experience can become a good one if handled well). If a single team is labeled as the primary keeper of the user experience, that absolves other departments from concerning themselves with it. User experience must be everyone's responsibility.

[3]

12 Qualities of Effective Design Organizations

In 2011, things began to turn around for NBA basketball team the Golden State Warriors. After years of apathetic leadership and poor performance, new owners made big moves, trading perceived franchise player Monta Ellis for Andrew Bogut and hiring coach Mark Jackson. The next couple of years saw more talent acquisition, such that by 2013–2014, the team had its core roster: Stephen Curry, Klay Thompson, Harrison Barnes, Draymond Green, Andre Iguodala, and Andrew Bogut. And even though they won 50 games for the first time in 20 years, they lost in the first round of the playoffs. Internal turmoil tore up the coaching staff, as Mark Jackson's approach seemed to be one of "my way or the highway"—assistants who disagreed with him were let go, and players were pitted against each other. After the playoffs, Mark Jackson was fired, to be replaced by Steve Kerr, who installed a new coaching staff, and a much more inclusive and joyful management style that welcomed respectful disagreement in search of the best answer. Under such leadership, and with no significant roster changes, the Warriors dominated the league, winning 67 games and the NBA championship.

There are two lessons for any team. The first is that skill and talent matter. By making big roster moves, the Warriors made back-to-back playoffs for the first time in over 20 years. But talent isn't sufficient. The second lesson is that to get the most out of a team requires sensitive management, visionary leadership, and well-run operations. Design teams often suffer in this second area because, compared with other corporate functions like engineering and marketing, design is newer and its appreciation is less sophisticated. This nascency means that (a) most people in an organization have never worked with a truly effective design team, and (b) most designers haven't been part of fully actualized teams, and so they don't know what they need in order to realize their own potential.

Many design teams have the raw talent to realize the expanded role outlined in the prior chapter, but don't yet have the maturity to embrace it. A design team's output is the result not only of their skill, but the sophistication and sensitivity of how they operate. In this chapter, we present a set of qualities of effective design organizations. Assessing a team's performance against each of these qualities clarifies opportunities for improvement.

The qualities are broken up into three groups: Foundation, Output, and Management (Table 3-1). The Foundation outlines the core concepts that drive the team's behavior, and explain its very reason for being. With a strong Foundation established, energies then shift toward Output and Management. These qualities are indicative of the broader creative/operational split that is required to sustainably deliver good design, and is a theme throughout this book. Output and Management need to be tackled in tandem, as they reinforce each other. Output addresses what most people think of when considering design—is the team able to produce quality work across the necessary set of capabilities? Management addresses the unsung and often overlooked aspects of actually running a team. To realize team longevity and continued broadening impact, it's imperative to treat operations as seriously as the work product.

TABLE 3-1. The 12 qualities of effective design organizations

FOUNDATION	OUTPUT	MANAGEMENT
1. Shared sense of purpose	5. Support the entire journey	9. Treat team members as people, not resources
2. Focused, empowered leadership	6. Deliver at all levels of scale	
3. Authentic user empathy	7. Establish and uphold standards of quality	10. Diversity of perspective and background
4. Understand, articulate, and create value	8. Value delivery over perfection	11. Foster a collaborative environment
		12. Manage operations effectively

Foundation

Often, in the rush to just get a design team in place and producing work, laying foundational components such as values, principles, and mindset is neglected. That leads to an unengaged team working without clear objectives, and efforts can feel frenetic and unfocused. Being intentional about the foundation leads to stronger work and more committed team members.

1. SHARED SENSE OF PURPOSE

Meaning and purpose are important for organizations at every level of scale. Companies have mission statements that orient and inspire their staff. Individuals have passions that motivate their behavior and decisions. Successful teams need a shared sense of purpose that establishes their identity and the impact they hope to have.

Making this purpose explicit supports design teams by serving as:

- A beacon that attracts talent excited by the purpose

- A rallying cry for team members as they do their work

- A signal to the rest of the organization of what to expect from the team

One way to articulate this shared sense of purpose is through a team charter. Charters can come in all shapes and sizes, from brief mission statements to lengthier documents that detail how a team operates. Start brief and expand as needed. Every design team is different, so no one charter will apply universally. We propose the following as a way to get started.

> We're not here just to make it pretty or easy to use. Through empathy, we ensure meaning and utility. With craft, we elicit understanding and desire. We wrangle the complexity of our offering to deliver a clear, coherent, and satisfying experience from start to finish.

2. FOCUSED, EMPOWERED LEADERSHIP

Successful teams, including design teams, have strong, formal leadership. Leaders have an intimate understanding of how the team should work, make decisions that benefit the team, and have the respect of the team's members. They then take this internal team understanding and translate it to the rest of the organization, ensuring the team is set up to succeed within the larger whole.

Because of design's nascency as a corporate function, design leadership often receives short shrift. With small design teams, it is common for a squad of junior-to-senior designers to report to someone who is not a designer, but instead in product management, engineering, or marketing. To a certain extent, this is acceptable—small teams are often at the start of their journey, and are part of a company that is in a more fluid state. Hopefully, the company just hasn't had the wherewithal to yet bring on a strong design leader, but knows that it ought to.

More frustrating are large organizations that should know better but continue this practice. An example was a Silicon Valley company (that shall remain nameless) that had four design directors as peers, each reporting to the VP of Product Management. While it might seem that design had real presence, in actuality none of the design directors were the head of design—that VP was. And that person was making decisions that affected the design team, even though he didn't understand the potential that design could be delivering.

A design team needs to be in charge of its own destiny, and this requires *focused leadership* with *autonomy* and *executive access*.

Focused leadership

We're using the phrase "focused leadership" to mean one or two people are running design and are from within the design organization—these leaders are not also overseeing other functions.

While design leaders must be attentive to issues of quality, a common mistake made by many companies is that they place in this role a design visionary, a creative director with big ideas and an obsessive attention to detail. A design organization is an entity that needs care, nurturing, diplomacy, and leadership. The skills that made someone a great designer or creative director are almost wholly unrelated to the skills that make them a great manager and team leader. Instead, this design leader's primary responsibilities will prove organizational, working with other executives to clear the path for design, and serving as a manager, mentor, team builder, and operator for the team itself, creating both a figurative and literal space where design can thrive.

For most organizations, a single leader suffices. In fact, this quality was originally labeled "singular, empowered leadership," because it's important that there is a clear line of authority within the design organization (and not a set of supposed leaders, all as peers, reporting into a non-design role). However, as the team grows, it might become necessary to split leadership into two—one person focused on creative matters, and the other on operational. There are many examples of such a split in other fields. Technology organizations have a CTO who serves more as a software architect, and a VP of Engineering who makes sure the team is running effectively. Publications have Editors-in-Chief and Managing Editors. In filmmaking, there is the Director and the Producer. And some design teams now have a lead Creative Director and a VP of Design (these roles are explained in detail in Chapter 5). This partnership model allows the creative leader to focus and more deeply engage on the entire journey and key initiatives while allowing the operational leader to focus on portfolio planning, capacity and hiring, budgeting, and an operating plan.

Autonomy

With focused leadership established, they must have autonomy over how the design organization works. Leadership's overarching responsibility is to make their organization as effective and efficient as possible, and given the expanded role of design, this will likely mean it doesn't conform to how other departments are structured or operate. This requires freedom to establish methods of practice, both internal to the design team and cross-functionally. And, finally, because design teams are always asked to do more than they have the capacity for, leadership must be able to prioritize their own efforts. For design to be seen as a truly essential contributor, it must be able to focus efforts on what matters, and say "No" to that which is not crucial.

Executive access

For design to realize its full potential, leadership must be only one or two rungs away from the CEO, and so must either be an executive or have executive access. If too far away from the "C-suite," then the politics needed to navigate the organizational reality of end-to-end experiences becomes extremely difficult. Such distance makes it easy for others to dismiss design's contribution. Executive engagement (whether in the form of sponsorship, organizational cover, or simple reporting structures) demonstrates the importance that design has within the organization. Such executive support will prove necessary as the expanded role of design inevitably upsets corporate "business as usual."

3. AUTHENTIC USER EMPATHY

Essential in design's ability to succeed is an authentic understanding of user contexts and behaviors. This goes beyond standard practices of market research and user testing, and toward deeper engagement with the lives of the people being served. Nothing beats going into people's homes or offices, and following them as they go about their days. While quantitative and marketing methods such as usage analytics and surveys provide data as to where things aren't working, findings from such efforts focus on optimizations and point solutions. Good user research, particularly out in the field, reveals a richness of understanding that you simply cannot get anywhere else. It is this work that ends up revealing a customer's journey, and inevitably, the experiential breakdowns that happen when people try to accomplish things that require them to unknowingly cross siloed departments in an organization.

The primary benefit of such observations is that designers develop empathy for their users, which in turns leads them to design systems that have real impact, and avoid solutions that will be rejected by the intended audience. A secondary benefit that can be just as important is when executives and other people with authority outside of design witness the results of such user research, whether it's the raw data (e.g., videos of people expressing frustration with the current situation), or the analyses that makes clear problematic patterns. When these executives ask how these breakdowns can be addressed, this is the opportunity to step up and show how design, specifically service design, can propose solutions that integrate silos.

4. UNDERSTAND, ARTICULATE, AND CREATE VALUE

After the dot-com bust in 2001 and the recession that followed, a cry heard throughout the software design community was "How do I demonstrate return on investment (ROI)?" At that time, most companies saw design as a cost of doing business, and something to minimize when times were tight. At Adaptive Path, we pursued this question through research that led to a 2003 report, "Leveraging Business Value: How ROI Changes User Experience."[1] While unable to identify a simple equation of x design leading to y value, the report stated:

> Our research revealed that using ROI and other valuation methods helps to evolve design competency within organizations. The valuation methods provide tools for developing and measuring a design strategy as a component of a larger business strategy: The ability to "value" user experience design makes it a visible and credible business lever on par with marketing, research and development, and channel strategy. As a result, applying ROI-measuring techniques to user experience investment decisions has a positive impact on how [design] teams are structured and perceived within an organization.

Given design's success in the decade-plus since that report, it might seem that the value of design is understood and such practices are no longer warranted. However, for a design organization to realize its full potential, its members must still be able to speak the language of value in a meaningful way. If designers shield themselves in the cloak of "creatives" as a way not to engage with the business, they will lose impact and credibility. Designers need to understand how their work contributes to business success.

Too often, designers practice design-for-design's-sake, where what's produced, however cool or innovative, isn't connected with the company's goals. Savvy design leaders embrace business value, realizing it can serve as a powerful input into the design process. Whether it's "hard" metrics such as improving conversion rates or increasing engagement times, or "soft" matters such as representing the company's brand in an elegant and appropriate way, these connections to what the company cares about are crucial for keeping design efforts on track. And when these business objectives are paired with authentic user empathy, new means of value creation can emerge. When design organizations propose ways to unlock new business value, their credibility and impact increases.

---

1   Available for download at *http://adaptivepath.org/ideas/leveraging-business-value-how-roi-changes-user-experience1/.*

Output

We are finally at the place where most people begin when thinking about design—making stuff! The following four qualities address the design organization's capability to produce sufficient, robust, and relevant work.

5. SUPPORT THE ENTIRE JOURNEY

"Support the entire journey" has a few implications. One is that the design team must have access to, and be involved with, all aspects of the customers' journeys. This will likely require change in how the rest of the organization thinks about design, because it means the design team engages areas where it had not been considered relevant, such as the high-touch practices of sales and customer service.

Another implication is that there should be only one design organization to undergird the entire customer journey. This runs contrary to a common practice, where companies often have two teams—a product or UX design team and a marketing design team. This is the legacy of 20th-century mass manufacturing thinking, where the way a product is designed and developed is divorced from how the product is sold and talked about. In a services world, this distinction no longer holds. "Marketing" and "product" experiences are simply milestones on the same customer journey. Also, whereas traditional marketing design was delivered through media (publications, broadcast, billboards) and product design was for a thing placed on a retail shelf, in a world of connected software, the platform for many marketing and product experiences has converged in digital realms such as email, web, and mobile. Granted, there are efforts particular to specific media—users don't interact with products on a billboard—but those are relatively few, and diminishing. Companies beholden to the archaic "marketing" and "product" distinctions also get in the way of new opportunities, such as the rise of "growth" product development, where what would have been considered a classic marketing function (acquiring users) becomes part of product development.

Given a single design organization invited to work end to end throughout the customer's journey, a third implication arises: the need for a vast array of design skills to address the totality of that journey (Table 3-2).

TABLE 3-2. The design skills needed for an end-to-end service experience

SOFTWARE PRODUCTS	HARDWARE PRODUCTS	ENVIRONMENTS	MARKETING AND COMMUNICATIONS
Interaction Design	Industrial Design	Wayfinding	Brand Identity Design
Information Architecture		Interior Architecture	Graphic Design
Visual Design			Information Design
Prototyping			Motion Graphics
			Packaging
← The Journey →			
Service Design			

Don't be discouraged by the breadth of this list—even most large teams aren't so broadly skilled. Still, the design organization must be accountable and responsible for the delivery of these design practices, whether they are done by people employed full-time, or external contractors and agencies brought in on a project basis. The design of the end-to-end journey is the sum of these practices, and having a single design organization ensures that these efforts cohere.

Facilitation: the non-craft design skill

A final implication arises in recognition of how overwhelming such a broad mandate can be. In a connected-software-and-services world, to render an entire journey is a matter of managing overwhelming complexity. There are too many moving parts, too much specialized knowledge necessary to fully appreciate a situation. Designers can no longer rely solely on the hard skills of their practice and craft to succeed. They need to facilitate the creative output of others throughout the organization, tapping into a resource often left dormant. If working in a hospital setting, get nurses, technicians, and doctors to ideate around their specific problems. In a call center, have the customer service representatives pitch how they think things should be. The point isn't to be bound to the input from other functions—the design organization still has the crucial responsibility of refining, honing, and executing these ideas. But realize that the problems we're solving are too big for any one team to have a complete handle on.

6. DELIVER AT ALL LEVELS OF SCALE

For the team to deliver to its potential, it must operate across a range not only of skills, but of conceptual scale, from the "big picture" down to the pixel and pica. Imagine a conceptual scale that spans a product and services view from 10,000 feet to 1 foot, and place design work along that scale (Figure 3-3).

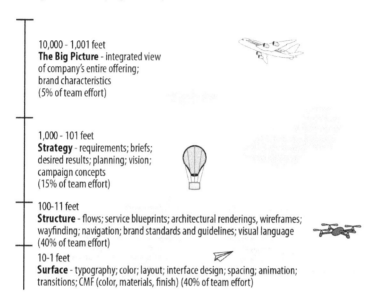

10,000 - 1,001 feet
The Big Picture - integrated view
of company's entire offering;
brand characteristics
(5% of team effort)

1,000 - 101 feet
Strategy - requirements; briefs;
desired results; planning; vision;
campaign concepts
(15% of team effort)

100-11 feet
Structure - flows; service blueprints; architectural renderings, wireframes;
wayfinding; navigation; brand standards and guidelines; visual language
(40% of team effort)

10-1 feet
Surface - typography; color; layout; interface design; spacing; animation;
transitions; CMF (color, materials, finish) (40% of team effort)

FIGURE 3-3

Design work is more than just what people see—design effort and artifacts inform product and service experiences at all levels of scale[2]

The relative effort percentages are not a strict staff breakdown—while individuals will gravitate toward a particular level, most will not operate only at that level. What the percentages show is that while the effort placed in the lower, execution-focused levels will far outweigh that which is spent in the higher levels, in order for design to fulfill its potential, it must deliver across all levels.

A design organization ought to be able to operate across these levels of scale regardless of its size. If the organization is just establishing an internal design function, the implication is that hiring a single

---

2 The levels Strategy, Structure, and Surface are informed by, though slightly altered, from Jesse James Garrett's *The Elements of User Experience* (New Riders, 2010).

designer is insufficient, because there's no way you'll find someone who can span all these levels competently. Instead, bring on two designers as quickly as you can, one who can take the bulk of the lower level work (spending 80% of their time in Surface and 20% in Structure), and another who can do some of that, but also engage strategically and across the organization (spending 60% of their time in Structure, 30% of their time in Strategy, and 10% addressing The Big Picture).

Newly hired design leaders brought in to run an existing organization can use this model to plan their next set of hires. When Peter was hired to run design at one company, he inherited an organization whose efforts mostly consisted of turning product managers' requirements into comps, and where user research made an impact only at the interface level. This immaturity was not imposed by the rest of the organization—product managers and engineers were eager for greater design contributions. Assessing the team's capability, he found that it was strong in delivering at the Surface level, mediocre when it came to Structure, and pretty much non-existent with matters of Strategy. Thus, design was getting in its own way when trying to have more of an impact. This drove Peter's decision to recruit designers who could deliver quality work at the Structure and Strategy levels. As they came onboard, design's influence grew organically.

7. ESTABLISH AND UPHOLD STANDARDS OF QUALITY

A design organization is ultimately judged by the quality of its output. What's tricky is that there's no universal definition of design quality. So while "high-quality engineering" is typically considered through quantifiable metrics such as reduction of bugs shipped, speed of performance, and service uptime, "high-quality design" is understood through subjective measures rooted in personal preference and taste. Sure, design solutions can have quantitative performance measures such as conversion rates and task completion, but they are insufficient in establishing quality. The ultimate assessment of quality often exists in the eyes of the beholders.

To overcome this, the design organization must be empowered to define quality standards for their team and their organization. Those standards then must be externalized so that others know what is being upheld. The goal is to take as much subjectivity as possible out of the equation, shifting design critique from a stance of personal preferences ("I really love this shade of blue") or a desire to stand out (the infamous "make the logo bigger") to an agreed-upon set of principles and guidelines that explain the team's definition of quality, supported by numerous examples of design work that demonstrate good quality with callouts as to why.

Once the design org has established such quality standards, they must hold themselves up to those standards, and not sacrifice. The rest of the organization will likely act in a way that unintentionally discourages quality. People outside of the design team don't understand what it takes to maintain a high quality bar, and design teams are asked to do too many things with too few people in too little time.

Too often, these teams try to do it all. Designers exhibit a couple of traits that can get them into trouble. One is a desire to please. Designers want to make others (clients, colleagues, users) happy. And so, when asked to do a thing, the default is often "Yes." The other is a revulsion at seeing work go out without designer involvement. Even when not asked to contribute, if they see that something might be shipped that wasn't intentionally designed, they'll try to find a way to take part, so that what is released isn't terrible.

These intentions are good, but the results are self-defeating. Teams get spread too thin, supporting too many programs, working overlong hours, and ultimately delivering subpar work. A design organization is only as good as what it delivers, and if it is producing crap because it's trying to do too many things, then the rest of the organization will associate design with crap. Design leaders need to wield the power of "No." Design work should only be done when adequately prioritized and staffed, and when there is time to develop quality solutions. This should not mean excessively long schedules for rumination and exploration. Good leaders know that there are points where design practice realizes diminishing returns, where further effort no longer leads to improved results. What it does mean is empowering the design organization to uphold what it takes to deliver quality, and to decline work that doesn't fit.

Many design organizations rely on process as a proxy for quality. This is a false connection. Critical thinking is essential for delivering great work, and an over-adherence to a methodology leads to teams making unthinking decisions. While a high-level process or general approach can help designers communicate how they work with other functions, insisting on a granular step-by-step process for every project engenders a rigidity that can actually harm quality. Design problems vary, and design teams should be familiar with a range of approaches and methods to solve them appropriately. "We must follow a user-centered design process" may sound like a good plan, but when any process becomes an assumption or accepted dogma, it becomes a crutch that replaces critical thinking. Instead of following a well-trod process, design leadership should make the effort to figure out the best ways to tackle different challenges, drawing from a broad methodological toolkit.

8. VALUE DELIVERY OVER PERFECTION

In a world where speed is often vaunted above all else, this talk of upholding quality makes some people nervous. So, "delivery over perfection" is meant to balance "establish and uphold quality." There's a quote attributed to Steve Jobs during the development of Macintosh: "Real artists ship." This recognizes that even the most masterful craftspeople, if they are actually hoping to have some kind of impact, must stop what they're doing and get their work out into the world.

Designers can have trouble realizing that delivery is just part of an ongoing process. For those who went to design school, every time they made something, they had one chance to get it right. And even digital design practices have their roots in traditional media, where once something is produced, it's in the world and out of your hands. This background encourages perfectionism, with a concomitant unwillingness to ship until you get it just right. With connected software and services, delivery should be frequent. By making delivery a habit (and not a rare event), the idea of The Launch loses its paralyzing power.

That said, continuous delivery should not be an excuse to ship bad stuff, with the notion of fixing it later. This is another place where leadership comes into play, because striking the right balance between quality and delivery is a matter of judgment. At IBM, they teach designers how to recognize when something is "ready," because with software, you're never really done.[3] That recognition of ready should discourage designers from noodling in the pursuit of an elusive ideal. Labeling something

---

3   From communication with Adam Cutler, Design Practices Director at IBM.

as "ready" may upset a team who doesn't believe the design is good enough yet, but ultimately the best way to gauge quality is not some internal assessment, but use by real people.

Management

A seriously underappreciated aspect of the long-term health of a design team is its management. Design leaders are rarely trained as managers, and lack familiarity, and sometimes interest, in the nuts and bolts of running their team. Without sound management practices, a design team turns into a hornet's nest of disillusionment, putting the quality of the team's output in jeopardy, and risking retention.

9. TEAMS ARE MADE OF PEOPLE, NOT RESOURCES

The department name "Human Resources" demonstrates how many companies think of their employees—not as people, but as economic units whose role is to contribute to a company's productivity. Design leadership must make the effort, which can run contrary to the broader organization's approach, to engage the team members as people. In return, those team members will be committed and engaged in the work for the long haul.

Three characteristics indicate a nurturing team environment, one where team members will be less likely to leave and will be their best selves when working.

Are team members respected as individuals?

A byproduct of bureaucratic work environments is that they encourage treating employees as cogs in a machine, not as the idiosyncratic people that they really are. Job titles imply equivalence and interchangeability for anyone with the same title. Discrete numbered levels are used to assess seniority and salary ranges. Org charts delimit access and authority.

Actualized design teams overcome such practices by treating team members as individuals, with all the messiness implied. They recognize job titles are imperfect, and two people with the same title may have different skills. That's OK, though, because everyone knows those people's strengths and weaknesses, and makes sure that they're set up to succeed. Seniority levels are seen as guidelines, not strict containers. Reporting structures are there for communication and mentorship, and do not limit anyone's ability to share ideas and have an impact.

While maintaining this individualistic perspective is challenging as the design organization grows, it's worth the effort. Designers, perhaps more than other professionals, are a sensitive, empathetic, expressive, and quirky bunch. Reducing them to labels and levels removes their individuality, blunting their engagement and, in turn, their work. Instead, celebrate their individuality. Let their freak flags fly.

Do team members work reasonable hours?

There's a difference between working hard and working long. The best work environments keep team members fully engaged during work, but do not expect people to commit 50, 60, 70 hours of their weeks. Overly long work weeks deliver a double whammy to designers—along with the obvious struggle with work/life balance, designers, as creative professionals, need to disconnect in order to recharge. Constant production and overlong hours stagnates work quality, as designers rely on what is basic and safe. Productivity can even go backward—poor decisions designers make while fatigued have to then be undone before the team can move on.

Are team members encouraged to grow?

A nurturing team is one that takes seriously the desire for its members to grow. There must be room for skills building and other professional development. People should not be expected to turn the design crank for 100% of their time. Managers must understand how team members want to evolve—do they want to deepen their craft, cross-train into other skills, learn how to lead?—and find ways to support them. There should be an explicit budget for continuing education such as attending conferences, workshops, or online classes. Great design managers provide little direction and lots of mentorship—they don't tell folks what to do, but teach them tools and techniques to help them figure out solutions on their own. (We delve deeply into professional development, skills building, and career paths in Chapter 7.)

10. DIVERSITY OF PERSPECTIVE AND BACKGROUND

A natural mistake made by design managers is to build a team of people who look and act just like them. It's what they're comfortable with, what they know, and because they have succeeded, it stands to reason that others just like them will, too. This leads to staffing a team of clones, solving problems in a similar fashion, restricted by groupthink, and limiting exploration by aligning on solutions too early in the process.

Key to successful design process is a period of divergent thinking, employing practices that open up a problem space. To achieve meaningful divergence requires that those doing the work come from a diversity of perspectives and backgrounds. Approaching a problem from a range of angles reveals solutions that may otherwise remain hidden.

Twenty years ago, there were few schools for software design, so people gravitated to it from a range of backgrounds—the founders of Adaptive Path had degrees in history, journalism, anthropology, and filmmaking. Now, as software design becomes further professionalized, with more schools producing more graduates, the risk is that the processes taught become dogma, leading to a narrowing mindset of how to solve design problems. Thankfully, counterbalancing this are mid-career programs such as General Assembly and Tradecraft, which attract people who had initially considered different careers. Avoid hiring graduates only from the same limited set of schools, and instead cast the net wide.

While design professionals are roughly split 50/50 across male/female lines, it's not uncommon for more technical product design teams to exhibit the same lack of gender and racial diversity of their broader organization. When Peter joined one company, he inherited a product design team of 11 men and 2 women, almost all in their mid-20s. Peter witnessed how this narrowed the team's worldview, with expectations that users had a degree of savvy with mobile and web conventions as they who were born digital. However, the company's audience was overwhelmingly female and middle-aged. And while a design team shouldn't necessarily reflect its user base, and user research can go far in engendering empathy for those different from ourselves, by having a variety of perspectives and backgrounds represented, designers are encouraged at all times to check their assumptions.

Also, on that team of young people, all but one were white. Race and ethnic diversity have long been challenges for the design industry, and very little has changed in the 20 years the authors have worked in the field. It's not an easy problem to solve, because even those eager to hire for diversity are hindered by the lack of diverse candidates. And diverse candidates might find themselves subject to unintentionally biased recruiting, interviewing, and promotion practices.

Making change will take time. Work with grade schools as well as universities, introducing design as an exciting, important, and inclusive field of practice to communities who might simply be unaware of it. Connect with organizations such as the Inneract Project (*http://www.inneractproject.org*) and the Level Playing Field Institute (*http://www.lpfi.org*) to support their missions of increasing opportunities for underserved students. When recruiting and interviewing, adopt practices that focus on competencies and results, using tools that replace casual assessment with rigorous analysis of candidates' work and behaviors.

11. FOSTER A COLLABORATIVE ENVIRONMENT

Realizing the benefit of diverse perspectives requires a supportive environment where people are encouraged and comfortable sharing their work, spurring collaboration that makes the final output better than what anyone would deliver on their own.

Every member of the team must demonstrate respect to every other member, or the openness required for successful collaboration will not emerge. Dismissiveness, insults, cattiness, and behind-the-back gossip lead to people feeling shamed and shut down, and cannot be tolerated. Instead, train the team to give authentic feedback and to deal with disagreements constructively.

Earning one another's respect is necessary in order for the team to "get real," because frank and candid critique and feedback are essential for upholding the quality standards. Greatness comes from the tension and collision of different perspectives (a concept known as "creative abrasion"), addressed openly and honestly. Design teams that favor politeness over candor will rarely produce great work.

Organizational hierarchy can stifle the free flow of ideas within a design organization—when senior people speak, it often stops the conversation. It's now become cliche, but it's worth repeating—great ideas can come from anywhere. Great design leaders encourage everyone to speak up, and, for themselves, wait to speak last, if at all. These leaders must also place their work alongside others, and accept others' critique with grace and humility.

The collaborative environment referred to so far has been figurative, but it also should be made literal. Great design work takes space— places to collaborate, whiteboards for sketching and ideation, walls to show work. And those spaces should be permanent, places where the team works and sees their work all around them. Not only does this encourage continual engagement from the team itself, such spaces enable people outside the team to quickly connect with the work. It literally demonstrates openness and transparency. And instead of having occasional big share-outs (that require preparation that takes time away from productivity), these spaces support frequent lightweight check-ins. This keeps the work on track, because if it begins to veer off-course, it is quickly corrected.

If physical spaces are infeasible (e.g., offices are simply too small, people work in a remote or distributed fashion), make the extra effort to create such environments virtually. Thanks to a whole host of tools such as Basecamp, Slack, Trello, Mural, and others, it's easier than ever for designers to collaborate online. Such solutions can never fully replace a well-stocked project room, and they require a little extra effort to make them useful, but with a little discipline they can prove quite satisfactory.

(In Chapter 8, we delve further into how to create environments that bring the most out of the people in them.)

12. MANAGE OPERATIONS EFFECTIVELY

The most underappreciated aspect of running a design organization is the importance of smooth operations (cue Sade). Just because design is "creative," it shouldn't get a pass in terms of running effectively. Much of what causes designers to stress in their work is the result of flawed operations. Symptoms include:

- Trouble coordinating internally, particularly around process, communications, and file management
- Difficulty collaborating with other parts of the organization
- Inappropriate staffing on projects and programs

- Lack of visibility into related workstreams or duplicate efforts

- Non-existent measurement

Such symptoms make people feel like they are spinning their wheels, expending a lot of effort with little to show for it. Ironically, though, designers often resist practices and policies meant to streamline their work, concerned with how it may inhibit creativity. In other cases, too much process will mask deficiencies in other areas, such as lack of a clear strategy, vision, or roadmap, and doing the work feels too prescriptive and constrained. Accelerated hiring and inadequate—or non-existent—onboarding further exacerbate problems (there's a section on onboarding in Chapter 8).

If done well, team members will learn to appreciate the ability to remain focused on the work, instead of being sucked into the work-about-the-work that insidiously steals a surprising amount of time.

Our Humanistic Agenda

Twentieth-century management practices were dominated by Scientific Management, which sought to squeeze the most productivity out of a workforce, and bureaucracy, which treated employees as interchangeable widgets. This mechanistic view of labor, where teams and individuals were considered solely on their output, worked in an economy dominated by the mass manufacturing of products. However, companies have brought it forward to the 21st-century challenge of connected software and services, and it proves tone deaf. Services hinge on relationships, and relationships occur between people. If a company has poor relationships with its own employees, how can it expect to have good ones with its customers? This humanistic orientation is even more important for the design team, as the very nature of their work exploits their humanity, from the empathy they draw from customer research to their design solutions expressing their perspectives.

Use these 12 qualities as guidelines for assessing a design organization. Have all the team members score the organization against each quality, and use the results to identify areas that need work. By making it an inclusive, whole-team activity, you ensure that responsibility for improvement is shared by everyone, further strengthening the team's bond.

[4]

The Centralized Partnership

CORPORATE ORGANIZATIONAL STRUCTURES ARE often employed without intentionality. People use what's worked for them in the past, typically some form of hierarchical bureaucracy, broken up into functional departments. Design teams embed themselves in these structures, modeling themselves on the other functional departments.

These structures, though, are products of 19th- and 20th-century industrial thinking.[1] Design, which has emerged as a primary discipline because of 21st-century concerns of connected software and services, will be stymied if it simply conforms to these outdated practices. To realize design's potential, design leaders must be thoughtful and intentional about how the design organization is structured and shaped.

Organizational Models for Design Teams

When the design team is small, say just five members, its organizational model is straightforward—it's the design team. The team is focused on a couple of key projects, and doesn't have to think too hard about how to tackle them—at that size, just do what feels right.

As the team grows, if something isn't done about this structure, everyone will report to one boss, and there will be one undifferentiated mass of designers trying to work together. That is not sustainable. The design team must evolve into a design organization, with explicit consideration around structure, project work, and cross-functional collaboration.

---

1 Many companies adopt organization charts unquestioningly, as if they are a natural aspect of enterprises. In fact, the first modern organization chart was designed in 1855 by Daniel McCallum in order to address the communication and coordination challenges of the New York & Erie railroad. McCallum's principles of management have been widely adopted, though were created for a much different era. For more about McCallum, read *https://en.wikipedia.org/wiki/Daniel_McCallum*.

Historically, there have been two ways that design organizations have typically operated: either as centralized internal services, or decentralized and embedded. Each has benefits and drawbacks, which we'll explore in some detail. We'll then introduce a third way, what we call the Centralized Partnership. Though unorthodox, it potentially leads the way for thinking about how functional teams (not just design!) should be structured to tackle 21st-century challenges.

CENTRALIZED INTERNAL SERVICES

Given that most companies' initial experience with design is by working with an external design agency, it's not surprising that when they first started building in-house design teams, the common organizational model was a centralized internal services firm, operating essentially as an in-house agency.

In the agency model, the organization is led by a director (who may have a design background, or may just be a professional manager tasked with overseeing the operations of the design team) who oversees a series of teams organized by functions such as interaction design, information architecture, visual design, usability, and project management. Each team is led by a manager, whose qualification was that they were the most senior practitioner of that particular function. These in-house agencies are typically placed inside a marketing organization (if the website was seen primarily as a marketing vehicle), an IT organization (because the Web was delivered on computers), or a newly created "digital" or "ecommerce" team.

This internal services group is seen as a pool of talent upon which to draw as needed by projects. Someone from "the business" (a product group, or a line of business, or marketing), would reach out to the director with a request for design work. Often this takes the shape of a creative brief that makes clear what is needed and in what time frame.

After some back and forth between the director and business representative, a project plan is settled upon, and the director then works with an internal resourcing manager to figure out who is available from which functional teams, and assigns them to do the work. That team tackles the problem in the given time frame (as varied as two days to two months to two years), and when the project is finished, the designers return to the pool, waiting for their next assignment.

Many companies go so far as to literally treat their internal design team as if it were an external firm, where the business unit requesting design pays chargebacks to the internal team, and where the business may opt to work with a design agency if it found it a preferable relationship.

Benefits of centralization

This form of centralization is so out of favor, it can be hard to remember why anyone would operate this way. That said, it's worth recognizing that it offers some very real benefits:

- Supports an internal design community and culture
- Provides clear lines of authority and control
- Allows designers to work on a range of projects
- Encourages a consistent user experience
- Create efficiencies in doing the work

From the perspective of the design team, the strongest benefit of centralization is how it supports the development of a design community. An internal services team, operating as an in-house agency, can replicate the focus and commitment of a design firm. This encourages the emergence of a strong design culture, as designers spend much of their time interacting and learning from one another. Designers have a clear sense of how they can grow their skills, and their careers. They have managers who can serve as mentors.

That straightforwardness in the centralized design team structure also provides clear lines of authority and control. For design direction and approval, there are no questions, as vision setting and decision making resides with the senior-most members of the team. This helps the designers focus on their work, because they don't need to worry about conflicting feedback. If there are issues or concerns, escalation paths are clear.

Also similar to an external firm, another benefit for designers is that they work on a wide range of projects, with different parts of the business, and of varying length and scale. This exposure broadens their understanding of how to apply design, and the variety keeps them engaged.

The clearest benefit for customers is that this approach encourages consistency across the company's designed experiences. A centralized team establishes design guidelines, and enforces them through the projects they take on. A customer knows what to expect regardless of which part of the company he is engaging with.

For the design team, these guidelines also lead to efficiencies in their work product. Once you solve a design problem for one part of the business, if another part of the business poses a similar problem, it's speedier to solve. The design team achieves quicker turnaround times on such repetitious challenges, and should be able to focus their effort on harder novel problems.

The finance department realizes the biggest benefit of centralization. By having all the designers on one team, there is no risk of redundant roles throughout the organization, keeping headcount costs down.

Related to that, if the centralized team uses chargebacks, it's very clear that design is something you pay for, not just some assumed utility like phone calls or printer paper. If a part of the business wants design, they need a good justification, and that will make them more serious about it.

Drawbacks of centralization

While centralization makes a lot of abstract business sense, when it comes to day-to-day practice, it proves problematic for the following reasons:

- Disempowerment and lack of ownership
- "Us versus them" attitude
- Lack of clarity around priority and timing

The gravest issue for designers is that they find themselves fundamentally disempowered. By the time designers are brought in to the project, the important decisions have already been made. Their concerns about assumptions underlying a brief are easily dismissed, because those designers will be gone when their part of the work is over. It's the people in the business who are held accountable, and with that accountability comes authority.

Design may be seen only as aesthetics and styling, or as one former client referred to it, "SUAC: Shut Up and Color." God forbid you actually conduct any usability studies, because any issues found will probably not get addressed, as designs need to be handed to the engineers at a specified time in order to meet the predetermined ship date.

This disempowerment leads to designers developing an "us versus them" attitude. They become disenchanted, nodding during meetings, but rolling their eyes afterward at the requirements they've been handed. They put in the bare minimum to get the work done, because their effort isn't going to be appreciated. And such attitude and behavior only reinforces the business's treatment of designers, leading to a vicious cycle of diminished expectations.

The business units requesting design get frustrated because they have no real control over this function. They have pressing and important needs, but they have to wait for the design organization to be able to staff a team. Other projects are given priority, and they don't understand why. When they finally do get design resources, the deadlines are such that there's not enough time for any creativity. They have to wait for internal design team reviews before work gets approved. And so the business feels that they had to wait a long time, only to get substandard work.

After this happens enough times, business units (or product teams) agitate for change. They want total control over what they produce.

DECENTRALIZED AND EMBEDDED

When a company realizes that its centralized, function-based organization is leading to delays, subpar work, and unsatisfying outcomes, a common solution is to reorganize into wholly staffed, independent teams, with all the capabilities necessary for delivery. This reduces overhead by giving these teams autonomy to make decisions that benefit themselves, with the expectation that if everyone is looking out for their best interests, that will bubble up and serve the interests of the company as a whole.

Design teams follow suit. Instead of a single design organization, designers embed within these decentralized teams. In technical organizations with decentralized product teams, one or two designers are grouped with a product manager and team of engineers (Figure 4-1). In more traditional organizations that are organized by business units (for instance, a bank that has units for checking and savings, loans, credit cards, and small business) teams are formed within those units. These teams have their own designer headcount, and fill the roles as they see fit. Designers work much more closely with business people and engineers, figuratively and literally.

Decentralized and Embedded

FIGURE 4-1

Designers (D) are embedded in each product/feature team ("Search/Browse," "Product Page," etc.), alongside product managers (P) and engineers (E). A director-level leadership team (DD-Design Director, DP- Director of Product Management, DE-Director of Engineering) overlooks all the efforts.

There might still be a design head, who remains part of the "corporate" or "headquarters" team, but that person's role has become more consultative and strategic. This design head helps the different teams understand how they can best embrace design, and helps executives understand the role design can play in the organization, but because of the autonomy given to the decentralized teams, no longer has direct authority over hiring and creative direction.

Benefits of decentralized design teams

The benefits of decentralization are realized immediately, and directly overcome the challenges of centralization. The benefits include:

- Development is speedier and iterative
- Designers are empowered and engaged as full team members

- Teams have greater ownership for what is delivered

- Output is higher quality

Because these decentralized business and product teams have been wholly staffed, they have freedom and speed that they couldn't achieve before. They no longer have to sit in someone else's queue. They no longer have to wait for approvals. They are in control of their own destiny, and design is part of that.

For the designers, instead of being brought in only after all the important decisions are made, they are now full team members. They participate throughout the product lifecycle, including the agenda-setting requirements development. They contribute to the strategy, and their perspective helps ensure superior product delivery. Their voices cannot be dismissed, because they're as accountable as any other team member. The "us versus them" they may have felt before falls away. They better understand the challenges that their team members face, and no longer see their job as simply handing off deliverables, but ultimately making the team successful.

Thus, this no longer feels like "work for hire," but instead something worth investing extra effort in. Being involved throughout the lifecycle means developing a real sense of ownership, and with that comes pride at wanting to do the job right. As they become more deeply aware of capabilities and constraints, their design process takes into account trade-offs. Unlike before, where their designs were altered by others after they had moved on to a new project, now designers are involved in the decisions all the way up to launch, and are better able to maintain the design's integrity. Post-launch, they can react quickly to refine the work and make it even better. The sense of ownership, deeper understanding of trade-offs, and close collaboration across functions leads to a better product than had been possible before.

Drawbacks of decentralized organization

This sounds like nirvana! What's not to love? While decentralized models work better in the near term and at smaller scales, over time the following kinds of issues arise:

- Teams are focused on one problem for a long time

- Designers become lonely and disconnected

- There is little cohesive design culture and community

- The user experience is fractured

- There are inefficiencies as efforts are duplicated

- User research is marginalized

From the designers' perspective, the thrill of shipping better work fades as they find themselves iterating on the same problem for a long period of time. There might be new features, but it's all within the same solution framework, for the same customers, and with the same people, and what was originally invigorating turns stale.

Related to this, designers begin to feel lonely and disconnected. On product teams, where there's often just one or two designers, they find most of their time is spent with people who don't really understand them, their craft, or their motivations. Maybe the corporate head of design has instituted attempts at a cross-team design community, but meeting once a month to share work doesn't feel sufficient. Designers are not sure how they should or could enhance their skills, and such efforts are discouraged by their team's leadership, because there's not enough time for those extracurricular activities. After a few shipping cycles, designers wonder, "What's next?" and "How do I grow?", and their career path is unclear.

While each product or feature, considered on its own, might be better than what had come before, when pulled together with adjoining products, all those decisions that made sense in isolation end up causing cracks in the overall customer experience. Customers get confused as they have to re-orient with new navigation models, new interface paradigms, new terminology. This trade-off of greater speed and autonomy might make sense in companies where the different offerings aren't really part of an experiential whole (think Facebook and its many different services, like Events, Photos, Messenger, Games, etc.), but in companies trying to deliver a most holistic experience (such as service industries like retail, banking, health care, and travel), this approach can make the overall experience worse than when things were centralized.

Decentralization also leads to inefficiencies. Instead of a single pattern for, say, displaying and interacting with a photo gallery, each team creates their own photo gallery experience. So not only has there been a ton of wasted effort, there's confusion on the part of customers who have to relearn how to use different photo galleries.

Whereas centralized design teams could conduct usability (whether or not there was time left to make refinements), it's often hard for decentralized teams to justify their own user research, beyond quick and inexpensive efforts like online user testing, analyzing logs, and inferences from A/B testing. If there is a user research function in the organization, it has likely remained centralized, which leads to little, if any, real impact.

Centralized Partnership: The Best of Both Worlds

Being centralized is too slow and disempowering. Designers enjoy the variety and collegiality, but ultimately feel stifled by their lack of impact. Going decentralized initially improves matters, in terms of both speed of release and quality, but over time designers grow restless and feel lost, and customers struggle with the lack of cohesion. Teams are thus tempted to re-centralize, but fear they'll just end up in the same place.

It's like the Kobayashi Maru,[2] but there's a lesson to take from Captain Kirk. There's a third way to run design organizations, one that is slowly gaining wider acceptance. There's no standard name for it, so we will call it the Centralized Partnership.

For most companies, it makes sense to have business and product teams decentralized. There are very real benefits of autonomy, primarily speed of execution, and decision making that takes into account the actual on-the-ground, day-to-day reality. It's a force that mostly does good. But it can lead to entropy, where the sum of these seemingly right decisions made in isolation leads to a fractured user experience. A centralized design organization serves as a beneficially opposing force whose holistic perspective can ensure coherence. It's not uncommon for multiple product teams to work on related, adjacent, or even identical stuff without knowing it. In the Centralized Partnership, the ongoing communication across the design organization makes this apparent early on, and those teams can figure out together how best to tackle it without wasting effort.

---

2 Nerd alert: the Kobayashi Maru is the Starfleet Academy battle simulation that tests how officers handle a situation where both choices lead to loss. Captain Kirk, the stud he is, hacks the test, creating a third way that leads to success.

The Centralized Partnership (Figure 4-2) attempts to realize the best of both the decentralized and centralized models. From an organization chart perspective, it is centralized, with all designers in one organization, reporting up through a single point of leadership. And recall what we stated in the last chapter under "5. Support the Entire Journey"— we mean *all* designers, even if they currently report up through different departments. Designers prefer this hybrid approach because it supports them in their career, professional development, and day-to-day working life. They aren't isolated on product teams whose members don't understand what they do, they collaborate with design peers who can improve their skills, and they receive guidance from mentors who help them chart a path.

However, these designers are not part of a general pool of resources that are assigned on a project basis. Instead, they are organized into skills-complete teams, which in turn are dedicated to specific aspects of the business.

Centralized Partnership

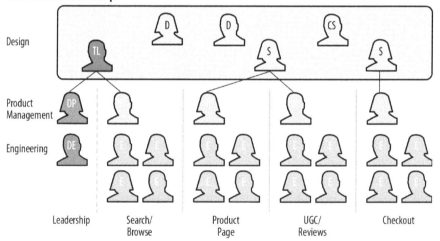

FIGURE 4-2

In the Centralized Partnership, there is a distinct design team that has committed connections to the different product/feature/business teams. The team includes a team lead (TL), senior designers (S), other designers (D), and a content strategist (CS). The team lead and senior designers have direct relationships with product managers (P). Experiences are treated more holistically, as the entire team understands the breadth of what is being delivered.

THE MAKEUP OF A DESIGN TEAM

Unlike the decentralized model, which orients on staffing design at the individual level (as many decentralized teams have only a single designer), the Centralized Partnership takes a team mindset from the outset. Just like flocks of geese are safer (thanks to their many eyes) and expend less energy (thanks to the reduced drag) than geese flying individually,[3] a gestalt occurs where a strong design team can accomplish much more than the same number of designers working on their own. A Centralized Partnership design organization is composed of these subteams, and the bigger the organization, the more teams there are.

What's described here won't be news to people who have worked in design agencies. Though many in-house teams are often dismissive of how agencies operate, there's much to be learned from companies whose sole purpose was to deliver the best design work. The philosophy discussed here was honed over many years of practice at Adaptive Path (where both authors worked), and has been successfully applied when brought in-house.

Teams range in size from 2 to 7 members. Seven people can take on a large program— consider a generous designer-to-developer ratio of 1 to 5, we're talking about a program that requires 35 engineers! If it seems the team should be bigger than 7, it's likely its mandate has gotten too big. Split the team into two, each with a sharper focus.

Each team needs a range of skills and the ability to operate across scales (Figure 4-3). While each team does not need to go as broad as the whole design organization, they should still perform well across the core software and communication design practices—research, strategy, ideation, planning, interaction design, information architecture, visual design, and prototyping. From the perspective of scale, the team will not likely be active in addressing the Big Picture, but should be able to operate across Strategy, Structure, and Surface. In the next chapter, we'll discuss the specific job titles, roles, and responsibilities you will find on these design teams.

---

3   Thanks to leadership and organizational consultant Alla Zollers for the geese analogy.

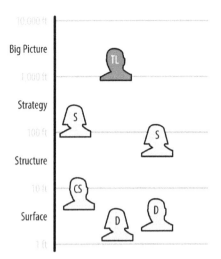

FIGURE 4-3

How a team's members array across the conceptual scale introduced in Chapter 3 (in the section "6. Deliver at All Levels of Scale"). Leadership maintains the broadest view, senior designers fill in the mid-tiers, and younger designers focus on the specifics.

Team leads for centralized partnerships

Regardless of size, each design team benefits from a single point of authority and leadership, an individual with vision and high standards who can get the most out of their team. This is the most important role on the team, and the hardest job to do well. Team leads must be able to:

Manage down

> Leads are responsible for overall team performance. They need to create a space (whether physical or conceptual) where great design work can happen. They must coach, guide, mentor, and prod. They address collaboration challenges, personality conflicts, unclear mandates, and people's emotions.

Manage across

> Design leads coordinate with product leads, business leads, technology leads, and people in other functions in order to make sure their teams' work is appropriately integrated with the larger whole. They must also be able to credibly push back on unreasonable requirements, and goad when others claim that the design team's work is too difficult to be delivered.

Manage up

> It's crucial that these leads are comfortable talking to executives, whether it's to explain the rationale behind design decisions or to make the case for spending money, whether on people or facilities.

Design leads must present clear arguments, delivered without frustration, that demonstrate how their work ties into the larger goals and objectives of the business.

In short, the best team leads are a combination of coach, diplomat, and salesman. And they are folks who, through experience, find they can span the conceptual scale from 1,000 feet all the way down to 1 foot. They oversee the end-to-end experience, ensuring that user needs are understood, business objectives are clear, design solutions are appropriate, and the final quality is high. To achieve coherence, they must integrate efforts across product design, communication design, user experience research, and content strategy. They are responsible for articulating a design vision shared not just by their immediate team, but their cross-functional partners as well. No wonder it's so hard to find such people!

It's important to recognize that team lead is not necessarily a people management role. In many companies, reporting structures and team structures are the same, but that doesn't have to be the case. If it makes sense for the reporting structure to be organized by function (product design, communication design, UX research, etc.), then a broadly skilled design team would be made up of people from across that reporting structure. Thus, the person leading a design team might not be the person conducting performance reviews or responsible for professional development.

ORGANIZING YOUR TEAMS

If these design teams were following the decentralized and embedded model, their mandate would simply be inherited from the business or product team of which they were part. In the Centralized Partnership, each team's mandate must be made explicit, and this is where the "Partnership" comes into play. With what parts of the business are the design teams partnering? Which product teams or business units? Do not consider this lightly. If an approach doesn't work out, and the design teams need to be re-organized, their efficacy will decline. Here are some guidelines to help figure it out:

Don't just mirror the product organization or business units
> In order for a team to successfully collaborate with others, it's important to understand how the rest of the company is organized. However, it's insufficient to have design teams simply reflect that

structure. Organizations grow and evolve over time, and the reasons for how they arrive at a particular structure are varied (e.g., acquisitions, firings, failed initiatives) and might not make sense for the team. A design organization that is not wedded to the structure of the broader company can help maintain a stable customer experience when the inevitable reorganizations occur.

Organize by customer type

A fallacy is to have designers obsessed with the products and services they work on. Product and service features are just manifestations of a user's relationship with a company. Instead, designers should be obsessed with their entire user experience. So, organize teams by types of users. Many companies have clearly distinguished audiences—marketplaces have buyers and sellers; banks have personal/consumer, small business, and institutional customers; educational services have teachers, administrators, students, and parents; and so on. When a design team focuses on a type of user, it can go very deep in understanding them, and that empathy leads to stronger designs that fit the users' contexts and abilities.

How this could work

Imagine work that supports a simple two-sided marketplace, such as eBay, Etsy, or Airbnb, where there are people offering goods or services, and people buying them. The product management organization for this business could have the following teams:

Growth Team

Acquire new customers, both on the buyer and seller side

Seller Tools Team

Tools for sellers to list and track sales of their goods and services

Search/Browse Team

Functionality for shoppers to find items in the marketplace

Product Page Team

Because this one page is so important, a team is dedicated to it, figuring out how to best incorporate imagery, copy, and reviews

Shopping Cart and Checkout Team
  Functionality to enable buyer to purchasing items

Reviews Team
  Solicit feedback from buyers and sellers about one another

These teams operate mostly autonomously, using APIs and other services to share data. They may occasionally communicate about specific requirements, such as the Search/Browse and Product Page Teams working with the Seller Tools Team to make sure the information sellers submit is workable in their contexts. Some of these teams focus on a kind of user (Seller Tools for sellers, Search/Browse and Shopping Cart for buyers), and other teams offer functionality that span users (Growth and Reviews).

These product teams report up through a VP of Product Management, but otherwise don't have much structure overlaid. An embedded model would place designers within each product team. While the Centralized Partnership could mimic that, with design teams organized by product, what's more appropriate is an independent structure overlaid on this product organization, supporting distinct buyer and seller experiences (Figure 4-4).

Keep teams focused on user types

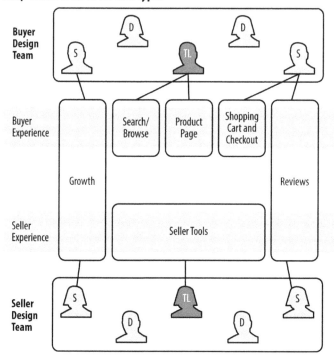

Design teams map onto product teams in such a way that they can support the end-to-end user experience

In this example, certain product teams, such as Search/Browse or Seller Tools, only collaborate with one design team, because their efforts are focused on one user type. Growth and Reviews, however, interact with both Buyers and Sellers, and so those product teams need to collaborate with both design teams. The senior designer focusing on Reviews is also familiar with the tools that precede Reviews on the seller's journey, and makes sure that the interface for Reviews flows from those tools in an elegant fashion.

This kind of organization may prove quite radical in certain companies. Banks and other financial institutions typically organize their teams around products or lines of business (basic banking, credit and debit cards, loans, mortgages, etc.) that behave as if in silos, and rarely coordinate. However, the same customer is engaging across these products, and can find the lack of coherence frustrating. Putting together a "retail consumer" design team that works across these products should lead to a better customer experience but will be difficult to maintain in the face of a company that incentivizes business units through their specific products' success. This likely requires executive sponsorship to demonstrate just how crucial a cohesive customer experience is for the whole company.

Organize by the customer's journey

If your company is successful, you'll need to grow those teams. Keeping in mind what we stated earlier that no design team should have more than seven people, consider splitting them up along a customer's journey. Using the Buyer Design Team from our simple marketplace, establish subteams such as Discovery, Purchase, and Post-Purchase (Figure 4-5).

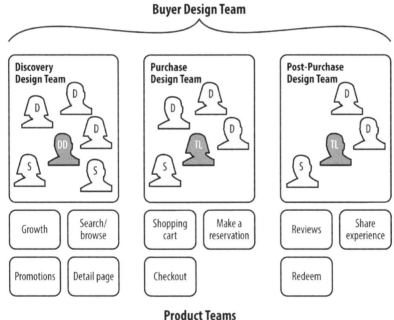

FIGURE 4-5

Three smaller design teams (Discovery, Purchase, and Post-Purchase) make up the larger Buyer Design Team

This approach to design team organization disregards whether the product or business teams are organized this way. Organizing by the journey allows each team to shift focus from features (search, browse, booking) to the overall experience, and the design work on those features will fit within the broader whole.

These specific teams roll up into a broader "Buyer Design Team." There is a director of this team (who, in this case, also serves as the lead for the Discovery design team), and team leads for each of the other teams. While all of these smaller teams mostly operate independently, it's important that they remain in contact, even if it's just a weekly meeting to share out what each is working on.

The teams shown here are a simplification to illustrate the idea of organizing by journey. In Chapter 5, we will explore the variety of roles and skills in design organizations and their constituent teams.

Commitment is key

As with any successful relationship, the key to making the Centralized Partnership work is commitment. In a centralized world, it's tempting to move people around depending on what seems to need the most support at that time. The strength of the partnership relies on dedication to seeing designers as members of that business/product team, to developing deep relationships across functions, and to understanding the business's goals, objectives, and challenges. Only then will designers earn the trust that allows them to engage in the empowered way of a decentralized team, working throughout a product lifecycle, and not be seen as mere stylists to make things pretty at the end.

With that commitment, designers then earn the social capital to push back on the business, either simply when something doesn't make sense, or when business decisions will affect the overarching customer experience.

That said, many design organizations realize benefits when rotating designers after a sufficient "tour of duty." Team leads must remain committed, but other team members might change teams after 9–12 months. Designers appreciate this, as it keeps their thinking fresh, exposes them to different styles of leadership, and broadens their skills and acumen. The business benefits because these designers, by bringing their experiences from different parts of the organization together, help weave a coherent customer experience.

Design operations must be made explicit

Traditional organization structures do one thing pretty well—communicate. When centralized, the command-and-control nature enables communication up and down the chain. When decentralized, the autonomous local teams are small enough so everyone knows what's going on. The Centralized Partnership complicates this, as the design organization likely does not map directly to the rest of the company, and members of specific design teams feel beholden to two sets of stakeholders: their business counterparts and their design leadership.

In particular, this is a challenge for longer-term planning. In a decentralized setup, business teams are responsible for their own designers, and so budget and plan accordingly. With the Centralized Partnership, business teams, which otherwise have control over much of their own destiny, do not have their own designers. This can make them anxious. Quelling their concerns requires conversations about planning, staffing, and the means of collaboration. Such conversations can prove burdensome for design directors and team leads, who need to be able to focus on creative leadership and professional development.

To address this, the design organization needs an operations team, what we call Design Management (or Design Program Management). It is not a big team—you can get by with one Design Program Manager for every 10–15 designers. The charter of this team is to make things go and to ensure that the rest of the design organization as effective as possible. Their work is made up of two big areas:

Planning and resourcing

> Work first with the business or product team leadership to understand roadmaps, backlogs, and other forecasting of activity, and then with the design team lead to figure out capacity. If there's a disconnect between what the business team wants to do and what the design team can handle, this then gets addressed through adding headcount or bringing on contractors. If it's not possible to get more people, then Design Program Management spearheads portfolio prioritization exercises in order to make sure the most important work is supported.

The Design Program Management team is the prime coordinator of how the work gets done, both within the design teams and across functions. They talk with design leads to plan the best process for tackling a design problem. As best practices emerge, they codify them for all the teams to draw from. They drive conversations for standardizing tool use—Photoshop or Sketch? Dropbox or Box? Hipchat or Slack?

This is explicitly not project management although many of the responsibilities are built off a strong project management foundation. Project management should be cross-functional, coordinating across the different disciplines needed to deliver. Though Design Program Managers are often in conversation with the delivery people (whether they're called agile coaches, project managers, or delivery managers), they themselves are not responsible for delivery. Within a design team, that responsibility falls squarely on the design lead. This means design leads must do some of their own lightweight project management.

Where Does the Design Organization Report?

If you put more than two design leaders in a room and ask them to talk about their work, it's almost inevitable that the discussion will address the age-old quandary, "Where does design belong in the organization?" The 1990s were a particularly painful time for this question. Many web design teams, along with their engineering partners, reported up through IT, the seeming logic being, "the Web is on computers!" IT, though, was seen as a department in service to the business, and so design by association had very little ability to influence product direction. The other typical placement was in marketing, as many companies primarily saw the Web (and its design) as a platform for talking about products, rather than a product experience in itself.

While we're mostly beyond this period, the question still remains. Many people advocate design reporting directly into the C-suite, placing it as a peer to product management, marketing, and so on. Given the expanded mandate for design we've been preaching, such placement makes sense in theory, but in practice can feel premature. The nascency of design in the enterprise means that it still doesn't have the critical mass or presence that engineering has, and also there simply hasn't been the time to develop enough credible senior executive design leaders. Perhaps this paragraph will be revised for this book's second edition, but there's a pragmatic reality that, except in very special cases (like Jony Ive and Steve Jobs), design just isn't quite ready for presence in the C-suite.

Because design's ascendance is primarily due to the rise of software, many design organizations report up through product management. Based on our conversations with industry leaders, that seems to work fine—teams that report through product are quite successful, even when those design teams are also responsible for design outside of product, such as marketing.

Some organizations don't have a single head of product management for the design team to report to, and in those instances, may report up through marketing, or even operations. It turns out that more important than reporting lines is that the design team:

- Is a single operating entity

- Has a mandate to infuse their work through the entire customer experience

- Has leadership empowered to shape the team and its activities to deliver on that mandate

NEW PROBLEMS WARRANT NEW ORGANIZATIONAL MODELS

The hierarchical, command-and-control organizational model that served business so well in the 19th and 20th centuries is proving ill-suited to the concerns of a connected-software-and-services economy. Most companies are simply ignoring this, applying outdated approaches and hoping for the best. Some who have accepted the contemporary reality are becoming radically decentralized, or "podular" as Dave Gray put it in his book *The Connected Company* (O'Reilly, 2014). And while this allows them to operate with uncommon speed, these podular companies typically have trouble maintaining coherent user experiences.

The hub-and-spoke qualities of the Centralized Partnership provide a strong centralized foundation (the hub) upon which to build, but give greater freedom to the teams (the spokes) in their execution to address the challenges under their purview. The push-and-pull between these forces creates a productive tension that keeps the whole organization moving forward without spinning out of control. This organizational model might just prove foundational not just for design, but for all functions within connected-software-and-services companies.

[5]

Roles and Team Composition

So far in this book, we have been vague about the people who make up the design organization, mostly lumping them under the term "designers." Roles, responsibilities, and job titles don't exist in a vacuum, but respond to the nature and needs of the organization. Explaining the Centralized Partnership was necessary before digging into our role definitions.

Design roles are notorious for their confusing titles and responsibilities. Should you hire a UX Designer? A UI Designer? UX/UI Designer? An Interaction Designer? A Product Designer? A Visual Interface Designer? Maybe an Information Architect? Design for marketing is a little more mature, but still suffers from label mania—are you looking for a Graphic Designer? Marketing Designer? Communication Designer? Brand Experience Designer? And what about the team's leaders? Do you call them Creative Directors? Design Directors? Should you have a VP of Design? What is a "Head of Design"? What does that person do?

Though frustrating in practice, this confusion speaks to a dynamism and vitality in the design profession that makes the work so exciting. To help temper that confusion, we propose a taxonomy of roles and responsibilities for a progressive organization that upholds our view of design's potential. It may at the outset be confusing, as it runs contrary to legacy practices that many have come to accept unquestioningly. Stay with it through to the end, and all the pieces should fall into place.

It's worth noting our antipathy toward job titles. Job titles exist to make company operations easier. Instead of accepting the messiness of individual people, companies operate at a level of abstraction and treat everyone with the same title the same. Such bureaucratic practices support a 20th-century need to operate at scale, but remove the humanity necessary in a 21st-century services-based economy. In reality, just because two people have the same title doesn't mean they are interchangeable. Nor does any title describe the totality of what any person does.

Titles are useful as you plan to build the team and don't know who the specific members are. You will need to shape your organization in the abstract, when asking for headcount, opening requisitions, and recruiting and hiring (discussed in the next chapter). In defining the roles that make up a design organization, our bias is toward generalization over specialization. Titles that are too specific become straitjackets, confining people to a limited set of duties, encouraging a bureaucratic mindset that employees are cogs in a machine. While generalist titles might feel uncertain, they provide wiggle room that allows for career growth, and encourage dealing with those who have these titles as people, not labels.

Individual Contributors

The bulk of the team are practitioners, individuals rolling up their sleeves and getting the work done. The first four roles are core to pretty much any design team:

- Product Designer

- Communication Designer

- User Experience Researcher

- Design Program Manager

Whether a design team includes the next three roles is a matter of size, industry, and the problems being solved:

- Service Designer

- Content Strategist

- Creative Technologist

Each of these roles contains a range of experience. For now, we're not distinguishing between junior and senior practitioners. Their basic responsibilities do not change in type, only as a matter of degree. In Chapter 7, when we delve into professional development, such distinctions will prove crucial for articulating career paths.

PRODUCT DESIGNER

In the 1990s, when the authors entered this field, the standard model was to split software design into two camps: Interaction (or UX) Designers and Visual (or UI) Designers. Using the conceptual scale introduced in Chapter 3, the former are responsible for Structure (workflows and wireframes) and the latter for Surface (layout, colors, typography, iconography). At that time, visual designers were typically people with print design backgrounds, and interaction designers were either people with computer science backgrounds, who studied human–computer interaction (HCI), or people who lacked formal design training but were comfortable thinking in systems and structures.

With subsequent professional generations have emerged software design natives, some practicing the craft as early as high school, and colleges now offer degrees in programs that develop both Structure and Surface skills. However, many current design teams retain the old split, which leaves designers who want to do it all feeling constrained by job titles that tie them to a specific practice. In particular, Visual Designers often feel that their role has been reduced to "make it pretty," and many seek to move into Interaction Design, which is often treated with greater respect.

Partly as a reaction to this new class of more broadly capable designer, in Silicon Valley the emerging consensus job title for software designers is "Product Designer," sometimes specifically "Digital Product Designer." While we recognize the irony of promoting the title "product designer" after having argued so strongly that we've moved away from products and toward services, no other alternative captures the appropriate breadth, and is free from unfortunate legacy associations. A product designer is responsible for the interaction design, the visual design, and sometimes even frontend development. In practice, very few people excel at all these skills (they're so rare, they're called "Design Unicorns"), and that's OK. Teams have interaction-oriented product designers and visual-oriented product designers who can complement each other.

Using the generic "product designers," regardless of whether they are more Structure- or Surface-oriented, provides for team members' growth and agency. It encourages designers to bolster skills that they are weaker in and discourages others in the organization from pigeon-holing them into a narrow set of expectations.

The one caveat for "product designer" is that in some contexts, it refers to a person who designs physical products, with product design a subset of industrial design.

COMMUNICATION DESIGNER

Product designers are people who can interpret the complexity of software into a form that is accessible and understandable to users. Communication designers distill the essence of a company's personality into visual communications that connect with viewers. Product designers are expected to have a baseline understanding of technical issues and how they affect design; they're not expected to have any familiarity with non-digital design. Though communication designers are typically not as technical, they ought to be comfortable with design in both digital and analog media. These designers usually have backgrounds in traditional programs such as visual arts and graphic design.

All communication designers are not cut from the same cloth. While they share a foundation in core concepts such as layout, color, composition, typography, and use of imagery, how these tools are used can be quite distinct. The more analytically minded tend toward information design, using graphic design to communicate concepts and processes with an emphasis on clarity and understanding. Those who are more playful and stylish gravitate toward visual and brand design, where the objective is to communicate the personality of a company in an emotionally resonant way.

Structure and Surface come into play, too. Structure-oriented communication designers create systems, such as brand standards and guidelines, and tie together the presence of a complicated service— for example, producing maps, signage, brochures, and other material for a mass transit system. Those working on the Surface obsess about typography, imagery, the interplay between words and pictures, and how all of this tells a story appropriate to the brand. Those communication designers who appreciate Strategy bring their skills to bear to define brand characteristics and establish a vision for an entire company—think about Target's use of red and the bull's-eye logo.

In terms of titles, matters are not as fraught as they can be within software design. While "Marketing Designer" is quite common, it is too limiting given the reality of a services world. "Communication Designer" acknowledges that this person is focused on the act of communication but is not limited to a particular business context. While most communications are to serve marketing, there are product and service communications such as printed collateral, direct mail, packaging, email notifications, and signage, and wayfinding. Communication designers should be collaborating with product designers to ensure the coherence of this end-to-end experience.

USER EXPERIENCE (UX) RESEARCHER

While great product design can be the product of intuition, great end-to-end service design requires the deeply empathic perspective born of user research. In leading technical organizations, it is common that once they reach a certain scale, often around the time they have five or six designers, they bring on a dedicated User Experience (UX) Researcher to do everything from out-in-the-world field research to user testing of interfaces.

Given our aversion to "UX Design" as a phrase, it might be surprising to see the title User Experience Researcher. "UX Design" is not appropriate because it's too vague, and user experience should be everyone's responsibility. UX Researcher is appropriate, though, because this role seeks to understand the totality of the user's experience, and the insights drawn from such research will inform work across marketing, sales, product, and customer care, as well as design.

The key responsibilities are generative and evaluative research. Generative research, typically field research such as in-home observations or diary studies, leads to insights for framing problems in new ways that stimulate the development of innovative solutions. Evaluative research tests the efficacy of designed solutions, through observing use and seeing where people have problems. Strong organizational skills and keen attention to detail are required, as much of UX research is operational management: screening and recruiting participants; scheduling them; note-taking and other data collection; and analysis and organization of that data.

This role is also commonly called "User Researcher." We prefer "User Experience Researcher," as it sounds less clinical and vague, and highlights what about the user is the subject of study—their experience with the service.

Developing a dedicated user experience research function does not absolve others from taking part in research. Researchers who work on their own, delivering reports filled with findings in hopes that others take heed, will find their impact blunted. Instead, the UX research team should remain small, highly leveraged, and supportive of everyone else's ability to engage with users directly. For larger, more robust studies, involving travel or time-consuming observation, it might not make sense for marketing and product development staff to take that much time away from their primary duties. In these cases, UX researchers will conduct the work. But within an iterative design and development context, most research efforts should be conducted by designers, product managers, and even engineers, with help from the UX research team.

DESIGN PROGRAM MANAGER

As discussed in Chapter 4, managing the operational aspects of design is particularly important in the Centralized Partnership. This is often neglected, or it is assumed that the design leaders can handle it. However, when a design organization achieves critical mass, at around 10 members, communications both within the team and across non-design functions outside of it become significant overhead. It takes real, focused effort to identify priorities, define cross-functional milestones, coordinate schedules, timing, file and document types, and other operating matters. If design leaders have to handle it, they can no longer give appropriate focus to the creative matters under their watch.

Bring on a Design Program Manager, someone with the explicit responsibility to keep design operations running smoothly. This person's primary objective is to make the design organization as effective as possible by enabling designers to focus on the work. This means facilitating prioritization, identifying milestones, connecting similar workstreams, managing risk, streamlining communications, articulating standards for tools and processes, aligning schedules, and ensuring the team has the people and resources it needs. This person also handles the logistics of relationships with external parties, such as contractors or vendors. To succeed, a Design Program Manager cannot simply be a generic operations manager—they must have an appreciation for design practice and process, so they can appropriately advocate for design when other members of the team aren't there, and not commit the team to timelines and outcomes that aren't feasible.

The Design Program Manager is a peer to multiple team leads, supporting them and their teams in their work.

Design Program Management skillset

Design Program Management operates at a strategic level, where it introduces design as a powerful tool with value to both the business, in helping to differentiate the company from competitors, and to customers, through guiding innovative and human-centered products, services, and brands.

As there are many specialist and corporate functions collaborating to deliver a service, there is an exponential amount of interests to be considered and coordinated. Here Design Managers need to:

- Make sure that the processes related to design activities run smoothly

- Manage the interaction between designers and other functions such as product management, development, marketing, corporate strategy, recruiting, and so on

- Take care of the communication, planning, briefing, and quality issues concerning design projects and activities

Design Managers bring excellent communication skills, an understanding of design methods and thinking, empathy for the needs of all stakeholders, and strong managerial and influencing skills to make sure that projects deliver as planned.

A plethora of potential titles exist for this role: Project Manager, Design Project Manager, Program Manager, Design Operations Manager, Project Coordinator, and Producer. "Design Program Manager" has the benefit of being specific to design, and gets away from the clipboard-and-spreadsheets quality of "Operations Manager." It speaks to a broad, portfolio-level view that "Project Manager" and "Producer" do not.

CONTENT STRATEGIST

An area where marketing has long surpassed product development is the marriage of content and design. Since the 1950s, advertising firms have understood the importance of having art directors and copywriters work hand in hand, whereas even today, typical product and service design practice separates writing and design. The design team dictates form and structure, and the content contributors are expected to fill boxes with words. This is a broken approach. For most digital services, it's the content, not the design, that is of primary interest to the user.

Progressive design organizations include content strategists, working side by side with product and communication designers. And like their design colleagues, they may operate across Strategy, Structure, and Surface. At the level of Strategy, they inform the brand strategy, and interpret it as a content strategy that includes editorial voice and tone, as well as a plan for ongoing content development. Within Structure, content strategists develop content models and navigation design, and on the Surface they write the words, whether it's the labels in the user interface, or the copy that helps people accomplish their tasks.

We suggest using the more general Content Strategist label instead of specific roles of Copywriter and UI Writer. As it is with product designers, some content strategists will lean more toward the systems-level structural challenges, and others will be more comfortable writing the final copy. Instead of siloing these roles, keeping it general encourages the Content Strategist to expand their purview, and tells the rest of the organization that this is a serious role to embrace, and not just a matter of filling space with copy. When it comes to content in end-to-end service experiences, it's important to recognize that it's not just about "writing," but crafting a content experience every bit as intentional as the design of features and functionality.

SERVICE DESIGNER

Throughout this book we have advocated a service design mindset. Most organizations don't need dedicated service designers—product design leads, UX researchers, and communication designers can practice service design, employing its tools such as experience maps, customer journeys, service blueprints, and prototypes of new experiences. However, some service-heavy environments, such as hospitality, financial services, and health care, will benefit from individuals dedicated to service design. These team members integrate efforts across product teams into a coherent whole. Whereas product designers typically work within Surface and Structure, service designers operate within Structure and Strategy, specifying the design of a system that will deliver a great service experience. While craft is important, this role is more about coordination—the service designer works hard to connect with all the frontline people who will be delivering the service. At the outset of work, this involves facilitation and co-creation, coming up with solutions that will work across roles and contexts. When the solutions are deployed, the focus shifts to training and implementation, supporting people as they execute the service.

CREATIVE TECHNOLOGIST

Too often engineering is seen solely as an implementation function, focused on executing against a well-defined plan. Design teams benefit from being able to engage with technology as part of the exploration of design solutions. Prototyping helps designers quickly appreciate the experiential impacts of their design decisions. When designers are limited to static representations (comps, mockups, wireframes), they may propose solutions that do not "feel" right, and need reconsideration after being built. Better to uncover this as part of the design process, when the engineering can be rougher (i.e., not production-ready), and there's not a significant investment in any particular direction.

Many product designers have this skillset, which allows a design organization to grow for a while without warranting a dedicated creative technologist. Teams can also prototype using tools such as Axure and Invision, which don't require coding knowledge. But at some point, usually around 15–20 team members, it makes sense to have someone who focuses on this practice. At this scale, efficiency is realized as creative technologists can go deeper and work faster than product designers who also happen to code as a part of their job. Additionally, without dedicated creative technologists, a design problem with a tricky technological bent requires a production engineer to take time away from delivery and support this exploration. A creative technologist on the team allows others to focus on what they do best, and serves as a deep connection between design and engineering.

This role can get confused for another such connection, the Frontend Developer. While frontend developers work closely with design and can be quite design savvy, the role is fundamentally an engineering role oriented on delivery. The Creative Technologist is less concerned about delivery than possibility. They can be fast and loose with their code in a way that frontend developers cannot. Frontend developers ultimately serve the purpose of the engineering team, focused on performance matters of stability, speed, and working-as-it-should at scale. Creative technologists align with the mission of the design organization, using engineering as a tool to uncover opportunities for a clear, coherent, and satisfying user experience.

Design Leadership

While the individual contributors do the work of design, the organization's leadership expends effort making a space, both literal and figurative, where great design can happen. Also, they must evangelize the organization outside the design team, helping their peers understand what it takes to be design-driven, and repeatedly deliver great experiences.

- Head of Design
- Design Manager/Design Director
- Creative Director
- Director of Design Program Management

HEAD OF DESIGN

As discussed in Chapter 3, for design to realize its potential requires focused, empowered leadership. "Head of Design" has emerged as a title for this role, which works regardless of whether they are considered a manager, director, or VP.

Whatever the level, the Head of Design is the "CEO" of the design organization, ultimately accountable for the team's results. Their impact is the outcome of how they handle three types of leadership:

- Creative
- Managerial
- Operational

A Head of Design provides a creative vision not just for the design team but the whole company. They establish processes and practices for realizing that vision, and set the bar for quality. They contribute to the development of brand definition and experience principles, and ensure that those are appropriately interpreted through the team's work.

Their managerial leadership is realized through the tone they set for their team. What kind of work environment do they foster? How are team members treated, and what opportunities are they given to grow?

How is feedback given? How do they hire, and who does that bring in? Is the team encouraged to wear *lucha libre* masks?[1] The sum of these decisions defines the Head of Design's managerial style.

Operational leadership is a combination of very little things and very big things, all in the interest of optimizing the design organization's effectiveness. The little things are what the rest of the team sees, in terms of how communications are handled, which tools are supported, how work is scheduled, how team meetings are run. The big things happen behind the scenes, and involve interactions with a company's core operations teams such as finance, HR, IT, and facilities. These include opening requisitions for headcount, adjusting salaries to ensure market competitiveness, establishing employee growth paths, acquiring the necessary hardware and software, and claiming physical spaces.

A common mistake made by company leaders when hiring a Head of Design is to favor creative leadership qualities over the managerial and operational. They bring in a creative visionary with big ideas and a beautiful portfolio, but often those folks don't have the patience or mindset for the mechanics needed to actually make an organization run. Design team members struggle without good management, flail without tight operations, and end up far less effective than they could be. Admittedly, it's a challenge to find an individual skilled in all three forms of leadership. This role is the "CEO" of the design team, and thus, managerial and operational excellence are crucial.

As the team grows, the Head of Design will not be able to perform detailed duties across these three areas. This is the time to bring on Design Managers and Directors (for people management), Creative Directors (for creative vision), and Directors of Design Program Management (to run operations). With these lieutenants in place, there is still plenty to do. At that point, a Head of Design focuses on:

Recruiting and hiring
> There may be nothing more important in the organization than identifying talent and getting them to join the team.

---

1   Hi, Chris Avore!

Living the culture

Addressed in depth in Chapter 8, the culture of a design team is essential to its long-term success. A Head of Design not only establishes the team's cultural values, but demonstrates them every day through his or her actions.

Process and practices

Working with Design Managers and Creative Directors, establish a methodological toolkit, and make sure it is shared, understood, and used throughout the team.

Vision

Developing a "north star" for the company is not a one-time act, but an ongoing process of refinement and evolution.

Represent design for the organization

The Head is the primary voice of design inside and outside the company, sharing its work, evangelizing its success, and articulating its vision. Sometimes this representation means fighting for design in the face of policies, procedures, and bureaucracy that limits the team's potential.

DESIGN MANAGER/DESIGN DIRECTOR

Design Managers and Design Directors are the unsung "middle management" heroes of any successful design organization larger than 10 members. They typically perform double-duty, responsible for both creative leadership and people management.

As people managers, they are key in nurturing the individuals on their team, helping them realize their potential. This requires a balance of compassion when providing career guidance, and candor when critiquing their work and exhorting them to improve. Good managers know their success is inextricably linked to the team's success, and are comfortable with the suppression of ego this requires. Folks who crave personal affirmation and recognition will struggle as Design Managers.

Design Managers must also be skilled practitioners. To earn credibility and their team's trust, they show that they can bring it when it comes to design delivery. This delivery can exist at whichever level (Strategy, Structure, or Surface) they are most comfortable. But Design Managers, even Design Directors, are not free from the requirements of rolling up their sleeves and doing the work.

The difference between a Design Manager and Design Director is either a matter of scale (directors might be managing other Design Managers, and have a broader purview) or seniority. But the nature of their work is fundamentally the same.

CREATIVE DIRECTOR

Unlike Design Directors, whose primary responsibilities are managerial and team-oriented, Creative Directors are leaders whose primary responsibilities are creative, and even with "Director" in the title, might have no managerial responsibility. This role emerges in recognition of a couple conditions:

- As teams scale, it can be difficult for the Head of Design, and even the Design Directors, to provide exceptional creative leadership alongside their managerial and operational duties.

- There are brilliantly creative people who warrant leadership roles with authority, but who are ill-suited to managing direct reports.

A Creative Director works as a peer of design directors, and is responsible for articulating a creative vision and setting creative standards for the design team. Brand identity standards, style guides, experience principles, and other aspects that touch on the entirety of the end-to-end experience fall under this purview. In sufficiently large organizations, there may be multiple Creative Directors responsible for different parts of the service experience. For a marketplace, there may be a Creative Director each for the seller experience and buyer experience.

DIRECTOR OF DESIGN PROGRAM MANAGEMENT

As the design organization grows, the Head of Design, fulfilling the "CEO of Design" charter, spends more and more time addressing operational concerns. This takes time away from creative and managerial responsibilities, which can suffer without attention. When this happens, it is time to establish a Director of Design Program Management. The design program managers report to this person, who is now chiefly responsible for the effectiveness and productivity of the design team (as opposed to quality and creative vision). If the Head of Design is the captain of the ship, the Director of Design Program Management is the executive officer (as *on Star Trek: The Next Generation*, Commander

Riker was to Captain Picard), making things go, striving for smoothness in how the team works, and removing the logistical and procedural obstacles that get in the way.

Five Stages of Design Organization Evolution

The roles just defined are the players in the game. Now the question is "When do they come out onto the field?" The rest of the chapter depicts the evolution of a design organization, from the first hires to when it has dozens of members, and shows when those roles are needed:

- Stage 1: The Initial Pair
- Stage 2: A Full Team
- Stage 3: From Design Team to Design Organization
- Stage 4: Coordination to Manage Complexity
- Stage 5: Distributed Leadership

STAGE 1: THE INITIAL PAIR

Companies that start by hiring a single designer force themselves to work through a series of trade-offs. Should they hire for experience and management savvy, someone who can build out a team, but who might be overqualified or disconnected on matters of delivery, and be expensive to boot? Or hire someone strong but junior, who can execute rapidly and with quality, but places design in a role subservient to others? Should emphasis be placed on pixel-level polish, or more on the structural level of workflows and wireframes?

Core to the philosophy of the Centralized Partnership is to orient around teams, not individuals. When that is done, the answer to these questions becomes clear: "Yes." From the outset, establish a design *team* with at least two designers who complement each other (Figure 5-1).

FIGURE 5-1

The design team starts with a Head of Design (HD) and a Product Designer (PD)

If the organization is serious about design as a competency, starting with two should not be too much to ask. Two designers allows for leadership experience and output velocity, structural competence, and surface savvy. The senior-most designer is the Head of Design, a role worth establishing as early as possible. This person is peers with lead product managers and engineers, contributing to product strategy and definition, as well as getting their hands dirty with the work. The other is a Product Designer, focused on execution. Together they set a strong foundation for design within the organization.

STAGE 2: A FULL TEAM

As the design team demonstrates its value, it grows to meet demand. The next stage of development is having a full, skills-complete team (Figure 5-2), ready to tackle pretty much anything thrown at it.

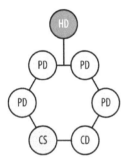

FIGURE 5-2
A skills-complete design team, with a Head of Design, four Product Designers, a Communication Designer (CD), and a Content Strategist (CS)

Along with the Head of Design and the initial Product Designer, three more Product Designers have joined. The specific makeup of each designer can vary. What matters is that there are strong capabilities in user research, strategy, interaction design, visual design, and prototyping, and competence across conceptual levels from the Big Picture to the Surface. The team also features a Communication Designer to address the growing need for non-digital design, such as marketing, packaging, or environments. Rounding out the team is a Content Strategist, working across marketing and product needs.

Everyone reports directly to the Head of Design. In day-to-day practice, this team tackles projects in units of two, so it can handle three distinct efforts at once.

STAGE 3: FROM DESIGN TEAM TO DESIGN ORGANIZATION

A single team of more than seven members proves unwieldy and hard to manage. Now is the time for organizational mitosis, splitting the team into two. This crucial step is where design goes from being a straightforward team to being a more complex organization (Figure 5-3).

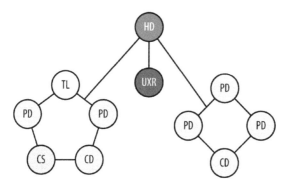

FIGURE 5-3

The design organization is composed of two teams; new roles include the Team Lead (TL) and a User Experience Researcher (UXR)

As discussed in Chapter 4, each team is skills-complete, and is committed to a particular part of the business. Continuing our marketplace example, one team would be dedicated to the Buyer experience, and the other to the Seller experience.

At this stage, two new roles emerge. First is Team Lead. This person is the ultimate creative authority for their team. The Team Lead will have come up as a Product Designer, Communication Designer, or Content Strategist, and is now expected to lead and oversee the work of their specific team. Team Lead is not a job you specifically hire—it's a role that an existing team member assumes. As shown here, they are not a manager—all team members still report to the Head of Design. The Head of Design also still serves as a Team Lead, because at this size it's important that they keep their hands directly in the work.

For products or services where the product team is familiar with the user base, this is the time to hire a dedicated UX Researcher. The UX Researcher is not part of either specific design team, but supports both. If the team's users are unfamiliar or the work is specialized (such as in heavy industry, or health care), it may make sense to have the UX Research join in Stage 2, and have a researcher dedicated to each design team.

Design teams vary in size and makeup. Teams focused purely on software product do not need Communication Designers. Some teams might have a larger scope and need more people to handle it. What's important is that each team have the complete set of skills needed to deliver in the partnership.

Moving into this stage tests the Head of Design. In order to achieve scale, the role becomes more operational and managerial. Some design leaders struggle with the mechanics of running a team, and some resist getting further from creative delivery. Such struggles, while understandable and worth addressing, aren't fair to put on the rest of the team, and aren't worth jeopardizing the organization's overall health. Many companies realize at this stage it is necessary to bring in a new Head of Design, one who is comfortable at this broader organizational level.

STAGE 4: COORDINATION TO MANAGE COMPLEXITY

Adding another handful of designers means creating yet another team (Figure 5-4), which signals a new level of complexity. Coordinating across three teams is an order of magnitude more difficult, requiring new roles ensuring end-to-end coherence, and keeping operations smooth.

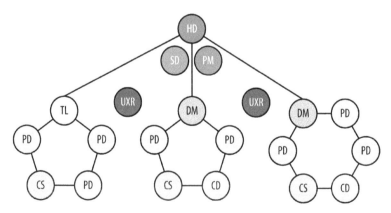

FIGURE 5-4

Complexity takes hold, requiring the coordinating efforts of a Service Designer (SD), a Design Program Manager (PM), and Design Managers (DM) doubling as Team Leads

With three distinct design teams, the risk of fracturing the customer experience becomes greater. To address this, and particularly for companies with complex service offerings, this is the time to bring on a dedicated Service Designer. Their tools, such as journey maps and service blueprints, provide a systemic framework to undergird the entire design organization's efforts. They also connect with frontline roles such as sales and support to ensure that design is cognizant of the full context of service delivery.

To handle coordination, communication, and planning across these distinct teams, bring on a Design Program Manager to focus on operations. Lastly, the team is too large to directly report to a single person. At the size depicted, the team should have two Design Managers to distribute the people management load. These managers also double as Team Leads.

STAGE 5: DISTRIBUTED LEADERSHIP

When the team gets to five or six distinct teams, simple management is no longer sufficient, and a true leadership layer is needed to keep the organization humming (Figure 5-5).

The structure of this organization is basically doubling what was shown in Stage 4, and introducing a leadership team. Design Directors behave like a Stage 4 Head of Design, providing creative and managerial leadership for the teams they oversee, and partnering with a Service Designer and Design Program Manager to ensure coherence and coordination. These directors, and their reporting teams, are committed to a broad but bounded swath of the customer experience— drawing from our earlier marketplace examples, one Director would be responsible for the Buyer experience, and the other for the Seller experience. The Design Directors have a new peer, a Creative Director, who bolsters their creative leadership and sets a quality bar for the whole design organization.

The UX Researchers now have critical mass to be their own team. They function in a microcosm of the Centralized Partnership, with a couple researchers committed to each Design Director and that director's teams. A Head of Research serves a purpose similar to the Head of Design, supporting the professional growth of the researchers, and maintaining a global understanding of research insights across all of a company's products and services.

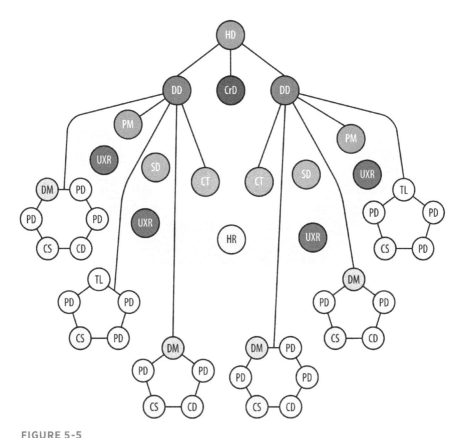

FIGURE 5-5

An organization of this size requires a leadership team. Introduced are two Design Directors (DD—each overseeing three teams), a Creative Director (CrD), and a Head of UX Research (HR). Also, Creative Technologists (CT) make their entrance.

Joining the org at this stage are Creative Technologists. One may have been called for at an earlier stage, but by this point, the efficiencies gained in having a dedicated design-oriented engineer are definitely worth the headcount. As they are still individual contributors, they report up through either a Design Manager or Design Director.

The continued evolution of the design organization beyond this point is mostly a matter of degree—it simply gets bigger and bigger. With specific design teams as the fundamental organizational unit, scaling is a matter of adding more teams, and augmenting them with other roles as needed. For every new design team, add a UX Researcher. For every three teams, add a Service Designer, Design Program Manager, and a

Design Director. The only major role introduced after this point is the Director of Design Program Management, who joins once the organization has about 60 people, and is a peer to the Design Directors.

WHERE TO GO FROM HERE

The evolution depicted here is simplified and generic, regardless of specific contexts, such as the nature of the business, the customer base, the internal power of marketing, product management, engineering, and many other factors. Those specifics will push the organization in particular ways. A company that is more marketing-heavy, or is reliant on collateral and in-person experiences, may have a greater percentage of Communication Designers. Companies delivering hardware may feature Industrial Designers on design teams. An offering that is less of a service and more of a tool will need fewer Content Strategists.

What holds, regardless of context, is the foundation laid out in Chapter 4: this is a single design organization for the entire company, with teams organized across the customer journey. This is a radical departure from the common practice to organize design within departments and by function, with a team of Communication Designers and a team of Content Strategists in marketing, and a team of Product Designers in product management or engineering. The genius of this system is that, because it is skills-complete at every level, it should work regardless of the organization's overall size.

[6]

Recruiting and Hiring

A DESIGN ORGANIZATION NEEDS DESIGNERS, and it may surprise design leaders just how much effort they must expend recruiting and hiring. It's not simply a matter of taking the time to hire top talent. Since the late 1990s, there has been a shortage of designers to meet demand. Even after the dot-com bust in 2001, there were always more positions open than designers to fill them. As we write this in 2016, the demand for designers is greater than ever, and that demand is only increasing. Given this competitive marketplace for talent, standard practices must be augmented with approaches tailored to the design profession.

Establishing Headcount

The process begins with opening positions to fill. Identifying those positions is part of annual planning, with mid-year adjustments as needed. The Head of Design works with their boss, their product, engineering, and marketing peers, as well as colleagues in Finance and Human Resources to establish headcount.

Calculating how many people the design organization will need is a bit of a black art, learned through experience and adjustments. Many companies use a "design to developer ratio." The logic of the ratio is to maintain balance within product development. Too many developers and the designers are either spread too thin, or some initiatives don't have design support. With too many designers, they get too far out in front of development, won't see the results of their work implemented any time soon, and spin their wheels trying to keep busy.

There is no industry standard ratio, and it varies by organization, depending on the nature of the software and services offered. When making this calculation, exclude developers who are purely backend. With a focus on "product" developers, whose work has some user-facing manifestation, a good ratio is 1 designer to 5–10 developers.

While balance is important, relying solely on such ratios places design in a position subservient to engineering, as developer headcount in turn drives design headcount. Instead, use the ratio as a secondary factor, an indicator of the overall product development organization's health.

The primary factor when figuring headcount should be annual program planning. The Head of Design and Design Program Managers work with each partner team to understand output, goals, and objectives for the year, estimate the resources needed to support that output, and get the requisitions opened.

This may mean that those partner teams need to lobby the finance organization on behalf of design. This proves particularly sensitive, and if the design organization treats this operational challenge without appropriate respect and attention, these convolutions will drive partner teams to cast doubt on the wisdom of the Centralized Partnership, lobbying to retain their own design resources. When handled well, the shared commitment between design and the partner teams grows even deeper, as the partner teams realize their fortune of having dedicated experts with far greater domain knowledge to handle their design challenges.

A problem arises when the source of funding (for example, a line of business) associates its funding with specific headcount ("For every $200,000 we give you, we expect our own dedicated designer"). This hampers the design organization's ability to manage resources as it sees fit, which is a crucial loss of authority. It's imperative that discussions with funding sources remain focused on *output* ("For this amount of money, we can deliver these programs with this impact") and not *headcount*. Avoid letting people outside of the design organization determine its makeup.

Recruiting

The recruiting and hiring process warrants the same attention and intention as the design of any other experience. Do not mindlessly succumb to your company's standard operating procedure.

Recruiting designers is different from recruiting other roles. Recruiters are often surprised to find that what works for other disciplines falls flat with designers. What follows are generalizations, so will not be true in all cases, but have been borne out over our careers in hiring. Generally, what we have learned is that designers want to do great work, work with interesting people, and get paid fairly for it, pretty much in that order. Keep in mind the following guidelines during the recruiting process:

Make the approach humanistic

While no one wants to feel like a cog in a machine, designers are more sensitive than most to feeling subjected to bureaucracy. Many recruiting processes feel like filing taxes or hospital visits—filling out forms, submitting material into a faceless system, facing uncertainty as to when to expect a response, shuttling from handler to handler. Recruiters need to understand that designers are a different breed of employee, and require a softer touch, a less aggressive stance, and a sense of connection throughout the process. Make sure to provide a human touch at every step in the process. Beware of adopting approaches that make it easier for the recruiter, but less personable. Given the competitive talent market, it's worth some internal friction and taking on extra work if it makes the experience more pleasant for the candidate.

Money is table stakes, but not a strong motivator

This one is a little tricky, because it can be interpreted as "designers don't care about money." While that might be true for a few, most designers want good compensation for their work, particularly where the cost of living is high. That said, throwing money at designers does not guarantee they'll accept an offer. In fact, many will find it suspicious, wondering what such largesse is masking. And while designers often struggle with financial matters—not sure how to negotiate compensation, unsure how to compare themselves to other roles—don't exploit designers' antipathy toward money. They will ask around, and if they feel like they're being taken advantage of, the deal is off. Commit to making offers that are fair for the market, and focus time and effort on those factors that will drive their final decision.

Emphasize the work to be done

For most designers, the primary motivation is the nature of what they will work on. Such inclinations vary widely—some designers love hairy content problems, others want to build complex enterprise software, and others crave sexy consumer experiences. Recruiting efforts should stress what makes the work compelling from a designer's standpoint. When Peter was at Groupon, the stock was in a bad place and the company had relentlessly negative media coverage. However, he was able to direct attention to the interesting design problem, which was to figure out how to leverage Groupon's success with daily deals and create other ways to connect shoppers and local businesses. Designers were attracted by the opportunity to deliver new features and functionality that created a marketplace, and the meaningful challenge of working with local businesses at scale.

Explain the environment in which that work is done

While some designers are dedicated to solving problems in specific industries, such as healthcare or education, many designers can root out what is interesting in any sufficiently complex problem. So when they're choosing between job options, they seek to better understand the environment in which they will work. Will they be expected to work on their own, or will they be part of a team? Are there opportunities to mentor or be mentored? What kind of authority and ownership will they have over their work? Is design respected within the organization? How does the company treat its employees? No one environment works for all designers. Be clear about its characteristics and let them decide.

Be honest, even frank—don't just tell them what they want to hear

Engaging with candidates reveals their preferences and desires. For design leaders hungry for talent, it can be tempting to tell candidates what they want to hear, to get them through the door and at a desk. However, if it contradicts what they then experience, the working relationship starts off on the wrong foot. That person is now less likely to suggest others to join, or may themselves be looking for exits, and the effort invested in bringing them proves for naught.

If a candidate makes clear they want to manage others, but there's no opportunity for that in the foreseeable future, don't tell them, "Oh sure, let's discuss that in six months and see where we're at." Whatever the pain in losing a great prospect, say, "I don't think we have a fit at this time," and move on. If you bring that person on, even if they have been told there are not management opportunities, every discussion will be clouded by that management desire.

Be direct and honest about what it is like to work there. Don't sugarcoat troubles. Don't dwell on them either, but acknowledge them and make clear the steps being taken to address them. The design community can prove surprisingly small and tight-knit, and word gets around. Bullshit is found out.

RECRUITING IS THE WHOLE TEAM'S RESPONSIBILITY

We all feel overworked. We all feel stretched too thin. We all want to focus on our primary responsibilities, and trust that others are handling theirs. Designers are already asked to do more than they have time for. So, design leaders are sensitive to taking their time away from their work.

But apart from the work itself, there is no more important activity for a team member than recruiting and hiring. Whom you work with plays a huge factor in your ability to succeed. Recruiting is time consuming, and the competitive talent market makes it only more so. Spread that effort across the team. The obvious benefit is that it lessens everyone's burden. It also strengthens the team's recruiting position. Designers like to talk to other designers, and so when team members are the ones reaching out and starting the conversation, it increases the chance of success.

Design leaders will have to help their team make the time to source, contact, and interview designers. It's worth it. Design Program Managers and staff recruiters should help parcel out the work so no one gets overwhelmed.

If the team simply cannot make the effort to participate, then it falls on leadership to bear that burden, even if that means deferring other responsibilities. There is nothing more important for design leadership than to ensure an appropriately staffed team. Too often design leaders get caught in a vicious cycle (Figure 6-1).

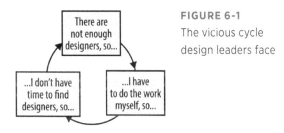

FIGURE 6-1

The vicious cycle
design leaders face

Let some work slide in favor of recruiting. The temporary pain is worth the ultimate feeling of accomplishment when the team is on top of the work wave, and not drowning under it.

SOURCING CANDIDATES

The first step in recruiting is sourcing. Great candidates can come from anywhere, and to build a design team in this competitive talent market, leave no stone unturned.

Schools and training programs

The last decade has seen an explosion of schools and training programs that teach software and service design. The advantage of recruiting from schools is that soon-to-be graduates do not have a professional affiliation and are eager to get one. However, hiring straight out of school is risky, as graduates typically have little to no professional experience, and only an academic understanding of design methods and skills. Before dedicating time to sourcing out of schools, the organization must be able and willing to do the hard work of professional development needed for graduates.

And while their numbers have increased, schools and training programs are not a sourcing panacea. School growth has not kept up with market demand, so competition for hiring top students is brutal.

Still, even with these caveats, school recruiting is worth the effort for many companies. When navigating this path, organizations must make a number of decisions to get the most out of the process.

Which schools?

Most programs dedicated to software and service design are found in one of three types of schools: art and design schools; engineering schools; and library and information science schools. The programs found in art and design schools draw upon classic studio design practice, and carry a variety of labels, including interaction design, media design, multimedia design, and digital design. Within engineering schools, the programs are usually found within a broader computer science program, and are typically called human–computer interaction (HCI), though some newer programs embrace the phrase "user experience." At library and information schools, particularly those that have rebranded themselves "iSchools," students receive degrees in "information management systems," but their coursework resembles those who have studied HCI.

Generally, art and design schools ensure a classic design foundation, including color theory, composition, typography, and the like, and encourage a more generative approach to problem solving. HCI and information schools have a stronger technical bent, with students learning programming, managing data, and cognitive psychology, and follow a more analytical mode of problem solving. That said, as design for software and services professionalize, and as employers make clear what it is they are looking for, the difference between these programs grows subtler. Any decent program teaches basics such as user research and analysis, the use of schematic design tools such as workflows and wireframes, graphic design, and basic programming and prototyping.

Along with navigating the art and technology divide, organizations must also consider whether to hire out of undergraduate or graduate schools. Undergraduates are more predictable—the overwhelming majority attended right out of high school, are 21 or 22 years old, and have no meaningful professional experience except perhaps internships. With rare exceptions, undergraduates will be projects, committing to a real job for the first time, needing guidance not just in how to work in design, but simply be a professional in the world. Graduate students have far greater variance in their backgrounds, from those who came straight from undergraduate, to others who fell into design practice in the course of their professional lives and decided to formalize their knowledge and approach, to yet others who were non-design professionals and are using graduate school as a way to change their careers. Hiring out of grad school means improved chances of finding capable professionals, even mid- to senior-level talent.

Given the dozens of programs out there, the primary challenge is choosing where to expend time and effort. Within the United States, there are a handful of top schools, including[1] both Carnegie Mellon's School of Design and its HCI program, IIT's Institute of Design, Savannah College of Art and Design, the School of Visual Arts, the Interactive Telecommunications Program at NYU, the University of Washington's

---

[1] ...but not limited to, so please don't send hate mail if *your* alma mater is not listed!

Human-Centered Design and Engineering, and the Rhode Island School of Design. Broadening to an international scope brings in the Emily Carr Institute in Vancouver, British Columbia, the Copenhagen Institute of Interaction Design, and the Royal College of Art in London.

It's not a simple matter of targeting these top schools. The power law applies when it comes to recruiter attention paid to schools—the top 20% attract 80% of the interest. Companies like Google, Facebook, and IBM harvest their graduates. Focusing recruiting efforts on top schools means playing in a highly competitive space, trying to get noticed amid all the noise. It's worth identifying one, maybe two such schools, and develop relationships with faculty and staff. Many schools encourage companies to sponsor their programs, and in return students work on real-world challenges those companies are facing.

Beyond that, those without the resources of a big aggressive company will realize greater returns when focusing on less renowned schools. How to navigate so many choices? One way is through the company's alumni network. What schools did people attend? Do those schools have design and HCI programs? Alumni networks can be remarkably strong, and people often have fond memories and deep connections with their alma maters.

Another tactic is to engage with local schools. They might not be the country's best, but they have the advantage of being right there. Less money spent on travel means more money to devote to other recruiting matters. Schools encourage relationships with local employers, and proximity enables deeper relationships. Schools appreciate any level of involvement, from guest lectures, to coaching and mentoring, to teaching classes. Developing a deep relationship with a school means engaging with students as they matriculate, providing a recruiting advantage for when they graduate.

Training programs

Accredited colleges aren't the only source of design students. Training programs like General Assembly and Tradecraft cropped up in an effort to meet market demand across technical employment. Kind of like graduate school, these programs are typically for professionals looking to make a career change. Unlike graduate school, the programs are much briefer—12 weeks or so—and focused simply on job-related matters, as opposed to the more rounded education expected from a full degree program. Given the greater variety of the backgrounds of people who enter these programs, graduates are more variable than those from traditional schools. Also, while plenty of these graduates can deliver quality work, our experience is that these programs turn out more mediocre candidates than those from quality schools.

Career fairs

Most schools have career fairs for their students to meet prospective employers. Out of any aspect of school recruiting, these events give the greatest return for effort, as they provide the opportunity to meet a bunch of students in a limited time. Reach out to the school's recruiting coordinator to get on the mailing list to find out about these events. Different schools schedule career fairs around the same time of year, usually late winter or early spring, which can be great for knocking out a bunch in a row.

Career fairs typically take place in some large room (a large classroom, a meeting hall, even a gymnasium) with a series of booths (or, rather, card tables), arrayed like a trade show floor. A common mistake is to staff booths only with full-time recruiters. While these people are preternaturally pleasant and have delightful smiles, students want to understand what it's like to be on the team. A strong booth has one full-time recruiter (to handle logistics and set up and track candidates), one design manager, and one designer. If you can only afford to send two people, favor designers over recruiters.

The design manager is there to give a bigger picture view of what it's like to work on the team, and to assess the prospective talent. The designer should be someone recently out of school themselves, ideally an alumnus, who can articulate the bridge between the college experience and the working world, and whom the students can closely identify with.

Make the booth attractive—we're hiring designers here! A banner hung limply over a table and a pile of business cards will not draw students. Consider standing banners, iPads with the company's work showcased, or even an HD display. Branded schwag is fun, but unnecessary—cheap-o sunglasses with a logo have swayed no one to work for a particular company.

Some career fairs provide opportunities for hiring companies to present to the whole student body. Prepare a deck that not only shows the work, but gives a feel for the company culture and environment. Have this deck built, and, even better, presented, by a member of your team who is a recent graduate, to strengthen that connection.

At the more competitive schools, some students receive offers on the spot. For those schools, seriously consider bringing a full recruiting team, as little is more frustrating than having met a great candidate at a Career Day, following up a couple days later, and finding out that they've already accepted an offer elsewhere.

If traveling, go for more than just the Career Day. Take time to get to know the students. Visit their studios, go out in the evening, and have fun. Avoid being the creepy old person hanging out with the youngsters,[2] but make an attempt to know them as people.

Internships

Hosting interns is a real company commitment, and shouldn't be perceived as cheap labor that can replace full-time hires. These internships are paid, and in competitive markets, employers will have to pay well. Because interns typically lack professional experience, they may require more support than full-time employees.

For companies that can commit to such needs, the potential rewards are great. Internships are perhaps the single best and most stable source of new talent for a design team. Bring on as many interns as can be comfortably accommodated. This no-commitment trial is a great way for both student and employer to understand what it's like to work together, and companies would be foolish to not take advantage of that. And these interns will go back to school, becoming ambassadors for the company. One single great intern experience can drive a broader interest in that employer.

Internships typically take one of two forms. One is for the intern to join an existing team and contribute in the flow of work just like any designer. The other is to set up a special project that takes place outside the normal flow of work, something too distracting for full-time staff to work on.

---

2   Cue Steve Buscemi, "How do you do, fellow kids?" GIF.

The benefit of the first is that nothing beats the actual, day-to-day experience of designing and delivering. The design team gets another pair of hands to chop wood and carry water. And the intern can point to a shipped product in their portfolio. The benefit of the second is that such special projects can be important and hard for the design team to otherwise find the time to do. For example, an intern may play with a new platform like Apple Watch or virtual reality. The uncertainty of the business value makes staffing full-time members unpalatable, but the potential of the new paradigm warrants exploration. This way, the design team gets to be involved in a strategic effort that could have significant ramifications. And the intern gets to drive a meatier project, practicing a wider array of skills than is typically asked from day-to-day work. The risk is that the work is either too secret to place in a portfolio, or never ends up getting produced after the intern leaves.

CRAFTING THE JOB POSTING

Many design managers deplore writing job postings. It's not clear they actually work. They all sound the same with their repetitive template of introduction, responsibilities, and qualifications. They're riddled with bullet points. The probable hire is someone who doesn't match the description. Why bother?

Given the competitive market, it's important to employ every available tool. At heart, the job posting serves a simple purpose: it is a signal of looking for talent. People considering new work discover a company has something to offer. Take the time to craft the job posting right. Avoid mindlessly following the template, and figure out how to communicate about the specific opportunity in a compelling way.

The biggest challenge for a job posting is the balance of general and specific. Too general, and people don't know what the job is. Potentially great candidates won't see themselves in the posting and won't apply. Many who do apply could reasonably figure they are suitable, even when they are inappropriate. If the posting is too specific, potentially qualified candidates who don't fit every bullet point may not bother.

The role descriptions from Chapter 5, which were biased toward generalism, are a good place to start. Add color to make the posting specific to what is sought. Call out the specific team ("Buyer Team," "Seller

Team") and project work ("dashboards, analytics, and other tools for sellers") that this role will be expected to deliver. State reasons why this is an interesting problem to solve.

When identifying responsibilities, be clear as to the type of work you expect the person will do. Will this person span from strategy to surface, or be able to focus on particular areas of the experience? Keep the focus on *activities* (conducting user research, designing structures, leading teams, coordinating across functions, crafting a new visual language, prototyping design solutions), and try to avoid discussing process *documentation* (personas, wireframes, mood boards, comps, etc.).

When articulating qualifications, focus on accomplishments and meaningful skills. Avoid numeric requirements like "5–7 years leading design teams," in favor of "Demonstrated track record of leading design teams that have shipped quality software across web and mobile." Instead of the uninspired and obvious "good presentation and communications skills," try "can frame strong rationales for design decisions that persuade peers and executives." Only mention tools ("Mastery of Adobe Creative Suite") in junior or execution-specific roles; if listed in more senior roles, candidates may assume the company doesn't take design seriously.

While the primary placement for job postings is the company's website, they take on lives of their own on job-related sites like Indeed, LinkedIn, and Glassdoor. Make sure the posting contains context about the company, its mission, and its values.

Apply an iterative mindset to the creation and publication of a job posting. Gauge the response to the ad, and tweak it to attract more desirable candidates. Approximate A/B testing by trying different messages, emphases, and ordering. Until the job is filled, revisit the posting regularly.

ONLINE SERVICES

Colleges and job postings will turn up some solid candidates, but will not be sufficient. To build a solid pipeline requires connecting with "passive candidates." This is the industry term for poaching. Reach out to people working elsewhere, who have yet to make explicit their interest in leaving. Many within the design community find this kind of cold-calling distasteful, reeking of aggressive sales practices. The thing is, it works. It's a slog, and most effort will lead nowhere, but when approached with savvy, it can turn up great candidates.

The primary means for passive sourcing are online services, and the 800-pound gorilla as of this writing is LinkedIn. To successfully source candidates on LinkedIn requires building a substantial first-degree network. Be honest and authentic. Don't become a living embodiment of the universal New Yorker cartoon caption, "Hi, I'd like to add you to my professional network on LinkedIn" (coined by designer Frank Chimero[3]). Your connections are your reputation on the system, and adding them willy-nilly weakens your network.

When looking to fill a role, comb your first two degrees on LinkedIn looking for possible candidates or people who might be able to help find candidates. With a robust first degree, the second degree will be too big to page through, so apply filters intelligently. Use the job title filter to find people with titles similar to the role. Location is important, too, but don't assume that the best passive candidates are nearby. If the role is in a "geographically desirable" location (e.g., San Francisco, Portland, Seattle, New York, Austin, London, Berlin), those overheated talent markets often mean top designers have settled into happy work contexts and are not compelled to leave. Consider looking for talent where things aren't so hot—many people in those areas are intrigued by the opportunity to move to a more happening locale.

The smart use of filters will provide a manageable set of profiles. When reviewing, look at job history to chart someone's professional evolution, both in terms of roles and companies. Accomplishments and achievements tell more than someone's self-assessment of their skills. Many designers on LinkedIn have links to their portfolio, underneath the "Contact Info" tab on their profile (we don't know why this crucial piece of information is buried). If they don't have a portfolio, that might be a sign that they're not looking. If the person's background is strong, though, reach out to ask for one. We'll discuss how best to reach out in the next section.

---

3 Frank wrote about his silly journey with the caption in "Hi, I'd Like to Add Myself to *The New Yorker*" (*http://www.frankchimero.com/writing/new-yorker/*).

Whereas LinkedIn serves as a general recruiting tool, there are a number of online services specifically aimed at designers, such as Coroflot and Behance. Perhaps the most commonly used is Dribbble, a show-and-tell space for designers to upload their "shots," and receive feedback from others. Though founded as a designers' community, the global hunt for design talent has turned it into a resource for finding designers. However, when recruiting off of Dribbble (or any similar service), be mindful of how work is represented. Many online portfolio sites elevate style over substance, and encourage a superficial appreciation of design.[4]

Reaching out to prospective candidate

With a set of promising prospects identified, the next step is to reach out and tell them about the opportunity. As the old Head & Shoulders shampoo ad reminds us, "You never get a second chance to make a first impression." This initial communication sets the tone, and if handled poorly, can turn the prospect off before there has been any chance to engage.

If possible, do *not* have a recruiter conduct the initial reach out. Given the competition for talent, designers are besieged by recruiter calls and emails. Most recruiters don't understand design, relying on obvious superlatives about "an amazing opportunity" at a "great place to work." Designers tune out such inquiries just to manage their own sanity.

Instead, have the initial contact done by a member of the design team. It's best for it to be someone at a similar level—junior designers reaching out to other junior designers, senior to senior, manager to manager. Designers usually enjoy talking to one another, and a connection from someone like that feels more genuine. If designers simply don't have time for such communications, then design managers and directors can handle this.

When reaching out, be concise and clear about the opportunity. Find a sweet spot between being too vague and brief, and verbose and long-winded.

---

4   This unfortunate tendency is aptly critiqued in the essay "The Dribbblisation of Design" (*https://blog.intercom.io/the-dribbblisation-of-design/*) by Paul Adams of Intercom.

Don't:

> Hi! I saw your profile on LinkedIn. We're looking for a Senior Product Designer, and I think you could be a fit for the role! Apply here: *http:// companyexample.com/careers/spd*

Do:

> Hi, I'm John Doe, a Senior Product Designer at CompanyExample. I saw your portfolio and really dug your work on that mobile ticketing app. I also noticed that we have Samantha Jones and Colin Yang in common.
>
> We have a Senior Product Designer role open here, to lead work on our Android App. We're looking to embrace Material Design, which you're clearly very familiar with.
>
> I really like working here, and would love to talk to you more about it, if you're interested. If not you, maybe you know someone I could reach out to?

Remember, designers are getting hammered by such inquiries. Give the person a week to respond. If they don't, follow up with one more outreach. Then let it go.

EXTERNAL RECRUITERS

When personal connections no longer turn up viable candidates, it is time to work with an external recruiter. These people typically work on a contingency basis—they are paid only when someone they found is hired (and there are usually stipulations that the person must stay at the company for a certain period of time). Using external recruiters is an expensive proposition—typical contingency fees are 20%–25% of the first year's salary.

The best recruiters are constantly networking, developing relationships with designers, and helping them advance in their careers. They know when designers are looking before anyone else. They are helpful when the hiring company has some tarnish. When Peter worked at Groupon, bad press and a low stock price made direct contact with designers difficult, as they would be turned off by the brand name. Those same designers will speak with trusted recruiters, who could make clear how desirable the opportunity was.

External design recruiting firms fall into a few different categories:

Big Recruiters with a "design practice"

Global recruiting firms like Robert Half and Robert Walters now feature design practices. Companies already working with such a firm for other roles will be tempted to use them for design as well. Never select a recruiter by default. Much of what works in recruiting for other disciplines does not apply to design. Make sure the recruiter understands this, and doesn't apply a one-size-fits-all approach. If they're approaching designers the same way they approach engineers, marketers, and salespeople, take a different path.

Creative staffing agencies

We won't name specific companies because, to be frank, these recruiters are the least pleasant to engage with, and have done the most to give design recruiting a bad name. Representatives from these firms hound hiring managers, relentless in their sales. They do very little filtering of candidates, primarily serving as a clearinghouse for people looking for work. The quality of the candidates is highly variable, and on average, subpar. Unless you have no other options in your area, steer clear of such companies.

Small design-focused shops

In our experience, these have been the best firms to work with. With just one, two, or maybe three recruiters, these firms provide high levels of service, getting to know you, your business, and what you're looking for. They also actively network with their local design community, and understand who is available and what they're looking for. They pride themselves in only proposing candidates who will likely be brought in to interview—no onslaught of résumés and portfolios to wade through. Given their higher touch approach and their smaller size, no one such shop will be able to help staff a whole team quickly, the way the Big Recruiters might.

But when you're looking for just the right candidate, and if you're willing to pay someone else to do much of the legwork, this is the best option.[5]

NETWORKING

A challenge for more introverted designers and design leaders is that a key to recruiting success is ABN—Always Be Networking. Pretty much every city has a local meetup scene, whether affiliated with a professional organization like the AIGA, IxDA, CHI, or UXPA, or a less formal "designers with drinks." Get on the mailing lists for these groups, and take the time to attend events and meet people. Making your presence felt is valuable.

Not only should leaders be going to meetups—they should also host. It is best to host at the company's offices, if there is a gathering space suitable for a presentation and it can fit a decent number of people. Inviting people into a space is a great way to advertise interest in hiring, and the design team can present its best self. When hosting, offer food and drinks, and make sure people have time to meet one another—don't make it all about a presentation. Be mindful not to sell too hard, but also don't be too shy—when giving over space to a local professional organization for an event, it's expected that the host engage in some self-promotion.

REVIEWING PORTFOLIOS

The most important representation of a designer's career is not their résumé, but their portfolio. Design managers end up reviewing dozens, if not hundreds, of portfolios for any role.

For those designers who do not have public portfolios, ask to see one. Any designer under consideration must have a portfolio. No portfolio means no job. For software design roles, be wary of static portfolios (e.g., PDFs). Product designers should be familiar with basic web technologies, whether it's handcoded and self-hosted, or using a service like Squarespace, WordPress, or Coroflot. It's more acceptable for communication designers to have static portfolios.

---

5   The number of firms doing this worldwide would be too long to list. We've had great experiences with Talent Farm (*http://www.talent-farm.com*), which focuses primarily on the San Francisco Bay Area, and Amy Jackson (*http://elegant.ly*), who primarily works with startups. Ask around and find the people in your area!

"Reading" a portfolio is a skill developed through experience. Hiring managers develop their own individual sense of what to look for, and this can vary depending on the role under consideration. The best portfolios should provide not only explanations of work, but should give insight into the personality of the designer as well. Be wary of portfolios that only show glossy images of the final product—design work takes work, and these cases should have a compelling narrative about the constraints and goals for the project, the role they played relative to others, and how they and their team arrived at the ultimate solution. However, a key failing of many interaction design portfolios is they overwhelm the reader with documentation, and while understanding the process is important, nothing is more important than the final result and the impact it had. Pay attention to the interface design of the portfolio itself. This work is solely under the designer's control, and reveals their personal design principles. An interface that attempts to be cool and innovative but proves onerous and obscure is a telling signal.

With practice, it's possible to screen a portfolio in 3–5 seconds. The bottom 60% are atrocious and not worth your time. They are easy to dismiss. A few, maybe 3%–5%, are brilliant, and while they might be fun to dig into, it's technically not necessary—this is a person to talk to. The next 10%–15% are good, and warrant exploration, to confirm the designer is aligned with the role. Trickier are the next 15%–20% of portfolios that may be solid, but for whatever reason are harder to parse. Maybe the candidate is more junior, and there's just not a lot to go on. Maybe they are coming from a different field, so they have a weak software design portfolio, but are strong in other disciplines. Whatever the factors, it's worth following up on these prospects, looking for that diamond in the rough.

The Candidate Review Process

Once a candidate has responded with positive interest, the process shifts into a formal candidate review. While there might be occasional deviations from the norm, we have found it best to remain faithful to this approach. Shortcutting the process increases the chance of bringing on someone who proves unsuitable. But don't belabor it. While it can feel like there's no harm in being extra careful, there are points of rapidly diminishing returns in this process, and overdoing it can both waste the design team's time and be a turn-off for the candidate.

With all the attention paid to the candidate's experience throughout this process, it's crucial to not neglect how it affects the members of the design team. Minimize their time investment for as long as possible, in case the candidate doesn't measure up—there's little as frustrating as spending a lot of time on a candidate who doesn't pan out. Do not exclude them, but do not make their involvement a burden.

INITIAL SCREENS (BY PHONE OR IN-PERSON)

These are typically called "phone screens," but if the person is local and willing to meet at a convenient time and place, it is often preferable to meet face to face. Conduct two initial screens. The first conversation is introductory. The candidate's résumé and portfolio should have already provided a base sense of skills and capabilities, so probe other factors. Get a sense of the candidate, their background, and their career trajectory. Share more specifics about the opportunity. Instead of addressing specific design aptitude, look instead for the meta-qualities that will make someone successful—are they articulate, pleasant, and passionate? If it feels like there might be compatibility, and if time allows, have the candidate walk through one or two projects and describe their involvement on them.

The assessment made after the first phone screen can be more forgiving. From the standpoint of career, experience, and personality, does this candidate feel like a potential fit? If so, proceed to the second screen. This screen returns focus to their work, skills, and execution. The interviewer should dig deeply, and engage with a critical eye. Have one of the design team's harsher critics conduct this conversation. The purpose is to ensure that only qualified candidates are brought in for the Day of Interviews, a time-consuming endeavor for the whole team. If after the portfolio presentation that kicks off the Day of Interviews, it is clear the candidate is a miss, the team is demoralized. They are committed to taking the time, as it's inappropriate to ask the candidate to leave.

DAY OF INTERVIEWS

If the candidate makes it through the fine-meshed filter of the screening process, the next step is to bring them onsite. As is typical for other roles, conduct a Day of Interviews, where the candidate speaks with a variety of people. To get the most out of the conversations, there are certain practices to include, and one unfortunately common practice to exclude.

Portfolio presentation

Begin the candidate's day with a 45- to 60-minute portfolio presentation. Everyone speaking later to the candidate should attend—this way the candidate doesn't need to walk through their work over and over again. This also gives interviewers a chance to appreciate the candidate's presentation skills, which are instrumental to a designer's success. When preparing the candidate before the Day of Interviews, encourage them in their portfolio review to share some personal background, to dive deeper on fewer projects (as opposed to presenting a little about a vast array of work), and to leave some time for discussion.

If the location of the portfolio presentation has room for more attendees, open the invitation to the broader design team, with optional attendance. This has two benefits for team members: they can engage in the hiring process, even if they're not conducting interviews; and it exposes them to new design work and how other people talk about it. A teaching opportunity emerges when design leadership's assessment of a candidate's work differs from their team members. This encourages explanations of what leadership is looking for, and helps team members develop and refine their review skills.

The interviews

Schedule a series of conversations with team members as well as key people outside of design. Limit the number of conversations to no more than six. A typical day for a product designer, content strategist, UX researcher, or design program manager would feature these interview participants:

- Potential design team peers

- The candidate's probable manager

- Product manager they would likely work with

- Engineer they would likely work with

- Design program manager

A communication designer would likely not speak to product management and engineering, but should definitely speak with people in marketing and copywriting.

For the peer interviews, feel free to have two on one. Such conversations can stoke camaraderie and gives the candidate a little more insight into whom they'd be working with. Keep the other conversations as one on one, either because of potential sensitivities (with a prospective manager) or because the people from different functions (engineering, product management) will have different avenues they want to explore.

Each conversation should have a natural set of topics, though the hiring manager will want to coordinate the interviews to ensure a complete picture develops. Make sure potential design peers probe across matters of process, skills, collaboration style, behavioral traits (how the candidate performs under certain situations), and personality and cultural fit. If the hiring manager conducted the first phone screen, then this onsite conversation is an opportunity for the candidate to take the lead and ask questions. If this is the hiring manager's first contact, they should probe on personality and cultural fit, and be mindful of professional development and career interests. Product managers will seek to understand the designer's "product sense," and appreciation for matters other than design. Engineers dig in to technical understanding, and also what it would be like to collaborate. Design program managers assess communication style, organization skills, structure of approach, and general fit.

Design Tests?

A topic of some controversy within product design circles is whether candidate interviews should involve some kind of design test or challenge akin to what happens in engineering interviews. Our firm, resolute response to this is "no." Design tests set up an unhealthy power dynamic in the interview environment, when instead you should be fostering collegiality. The context in which the challenge is given (typically narrowly time-boxed and with only a little information and little support) is wholly artificial—and so whether a candidate succeeds or fails is not a meaningful indicator of actual practice. There is nothing you will find out in such a test that you couldn't better learn through probing the candidate about their portfolio.

Coordinating feedback

This is an area where what works for the rest of the organization pretty much works for design. Interviewers need to submit feedback in a timely fashion (i.e., within 24 hours), making clear what they discussed, what their impressions were, and how strongly they feel about hiring or not hiring the candidate.

Even if the company does not otherwise conduct debriefs, where the interview panel meets in person to discuss their interviews, do so for design candidates. The newness of design as a corporate function comes into particular play in the hiring process. Many people, especially those outside of design, will not have interviewed designers before. Everyone benefits from understanding each other's assessments. It helps the whole organization as it figures out how to hire for these roles.

The debrief should also be timely, ideally the following day, but no more than three days after the interview. The panel should read one another's feedback before the debrief, or if they haven't had time, at the beginning of the debrief. Most debriefs will be straightforward—across the board thumbs up or thumbs down. Be careful of tepid approvals, though—if there are no strong advocates for a person's hire, that's a sign of something being off, even if none of the feedback is negative.

A challenge arises when a candidate splits the panel, where some are strongly positive, and others are inclined not to hire. Navigating this is among the most heightened and sensitive tasks for a design leader, because there is nothing more damning than a mis-hire, especially where there's evidence that not everyone was on board.

In most situations where there's a split, the easiest decision is the same as the right decision—do not hire. Given how costly it is to make a hiring mistake, "better safe than sorry" is often an appropriate strategy. But it is not a universal, and how this is handled is one of those areas that distinguishes design leaders from design managers. If a design leader deeply believes in the potential of a candidate, and can identify flaws in the rationale of those who object, the design leader should make the case for why an offer ought to be extended to the candidate.

There are reasons for rejection that design leaders need to be wary of, and call out if they are the only impediment to hiring:

Unfamiliar background or approach

Designers, particularly those with less experience, can be quite orthodox in how they evaluate other designers. They may be suspicious of any designer who doesn't share their background or approach. An atypical background (maybe they didn't study design in school), or unfamiliar approach (perhaps they don't use typical design tools, or they're unfamiliar with industry standard methods) can make panel members uneasy, because it's not how they do it, and they don't understand how other ways can be successful. The design leader's role is to remind the panel of what is most important—results. If an unorthodox approach leads to great design work, the onus is on the team to figure out how they might be able to incorporate such different ways into their team. In fact, a willingness to consider people with atypical backgrounds provides two benefits: there will likely be less competition for that person (because other companies will also be hesitant with the unfamiliar); and the incorporation of new ways of working will increase the team's diversity of perspective, enabling even better work.

Awkward communicators

If the interview process has one crucial drawback, it would be its reliance on conversations as the primary medium of understanding. The portfolio review mitigates this somewhat, but one of the things any candidate is being tested on when talking to people over the course of a day is how well they communicate. Many talented designers are not good oral communicators. It might even be part of the reason they got into design—being more comfortable with pictures than words. People who are awkward communicators (and good designers) often process the world differently than others, and that difference can actually make for a stronger team by bringing in uncommon ways of working and thinking. Also, communication and presentation skills can be taught and improved.

Candidate is a little weird

Maybe they talk fast or loud. Maybe they have some uncommon obsessions. Maybe they demonstrate unbridled enthusiasm or a lack of social graces. Whatever it is, you will interview candidates that are a little weird. Don't let that weirdness be a turn-off. In fact, lean in to your team's weirdness. If a design team can't bring weirdness into a company, who can? If people on the interview panel grow wary when candidates let their freak flags fly, reorient their thinking to the quality of that candidate's work, and whether they think the candidate will be truly disruptive (and not just a little strange).

REFERENCE CHECKS

An underused tool in the hiring process is the reference check. When the interview panel is split on a candidate, what better source of information than people who have worked with that person before? Reference checks won't reveal much about skills or capabilities (the portfolio does that), but should help in understanding what it's like to work with that person—their communication style, how they are as a leader or collaborator, whether they get along well with others, if they are headstrong, whether they are generally positive or negative, and so on.

Many people dismiss these checks because the references come from the candidate, and of course the candidate will only connect you with people who will give a positive impression. In our experience, these conversations can still be revealing, as long as you are specific in the information you seek. Don't ask general questions like "What's it like to work with her?" Focus on what came up in the candidate debrief, and ask specific question such as the following:

- "What were her strengths as a team lead? Her weaknesses?"

- "How did she help you in your work?"

- "How was she in working with engineers and product managers?"

- "Were I to hire this person, what would I need to do as her manager to help her be successful?"

Thanks to LinkedIn, mutual connections can be found that weren't listed as a formal reference. These "back-channel" references are more likely to be frank, and the feedback will prove more convincing to the interview panel.

Making the Hire Decision

It's now time to make a decision—will the candidate receive an offer? Roughly 90% of the time, the answer will be a clear "yes" or "no." That remaining 10% is where it gets tricky. The hiring decision might be where a manager has the greatest impact. So, about 80%–90% of the time within that 10%, it's probably best not to hire, no matter how badly the team needs to grow. It can be seductively easy to rationalize that extending the offer is the right thing to do. Hiring managers should listen to their hearts, even their guts, rather than their heads.

Sometimes the gut encourages a positive hiring decision that seems contrary to better judgment. Listen to that, too. The occasional risk is worth it, because the potential reward can be enormous.

It's important that the hiring manager have authority for making this decision. They should seek counsel from all around, but these folks need to be able to build their teams as they see fit.

CONTRACT-TO-HIRE

Sometimes, it is hard to let someone go, but an out-and-out offer is infeasible. Maybe the person is pretty junior, so they just don't have enough of a track record to rely on, but have shown some promise. Maybe the person is senior, and not quite suited to the role applied for, but a different role might be a fit. This is the time to broach the option of a contract-to-hire, where someone comes on board in a contract capacity (typically for three months), after which a decision is made to keep the person on full-time or to cut ties.

Extending the Offer

When the decision to hire has been made, work with the internal recruiting team to put together an offer. Make sure the offer is fair. Many companies use some service to peg their salaries with a market standard. Designer-specific compensation is the subject of O'Reilly's Design Salary Survey (*http://www.oreilly.com/design/free/2016-design-salary-survey-report.csp*) and Coroflot's Design Salary Guide (*http://www.coroflot.com/designsalaryguide*). Candidates are likely talking to multiple companies, and will probably receive multiple offers. Being cheap demonstrates a lack of commitment and investment in design, and a sure way to have a candidate turn down the offer.

That said, don't go overboard with generosity, either. Remember, while a fair salary is table stakes in a candidate's decision of where to go, offering more money doesn't necessarily increase the likelihood of their acceptance. Designers are motivated by other factors, such as the specific work they'll be doing, and the people with whom they'll be working. If you're able to compete on those factors, the salary can be market average and that should be fine.

In technology companies, or others who are competing hard for the best talent, equity is often a component of compensation. In our experience, if there is a need to increase compensation (for example, the candidate has received multiple strong offers), recognize that most designers are affected more by money than equity (whether stock options or restricted stock units). They often dismiss compensation that isn't hard cash, either because they don't understand equity, or they've been burned by it before. We've seen very generous stock offers rejected out of hand, particularly when other companies were offering cash components like bonuses. When explaining to a candidate the compensation calculation when it comes to stock, be prepared to be met with blank stares.

If someone other than the hiring manager communicates the offer, the hiring manager should reach out to the candidate immediately after the offer has been extended. If communication happens only through an HR functionary, the candidate loses their connection to the design team. It's important to maintain that connection, and to be available to answer any questions or address any concerns. Work with the recruiting partner to make sure the candidate is not overwhelmed with communication, and that all discussions with the candidate are consistent.

Ideally, the candidate accepts the offer, no questions asked. Practically, it's rarely so smooth. For whatever reason (multiple offers, contentment at current job, uncertainty about relocation, etc.), there will likely be some negotiation about the offer. The two most common sticking points are money and role. With money, if the candidate has a higher competing offer, work with the recruiter to determine the maximum counter. If your offer is fair, consider one-time expenditures that demonstrate your commitment, such as signing or relocation bonuses. If the candidate still chooses elsewhere because of money, they probably would not have been right for the team.

Often, it's not the salary but the role that becomes the subject of negotiation. The offer is for a "Product Designer" title, but another company is willing to call them "Senior Product Designer." Or they want promises of management or leadership responsibility that weren't part of the role definition. These are potentially sensitive cultural matters, and it's important to hold firm. It's better to be up-front and not see a hire through than to prevaricate and disappoint them later. Giving someone an inflated title in order to land them sends ripples through the design team—current staff members wonder why someone with less experience has a more senior title, there's confusion around performance reviews about how to judge the candidate, and the candidate has an inflated sense of entitlement. If someone is not senior, tell them that, and be clear as to why. If a role definition proves make-or-break in negotiations, walk away from such discussions with head held high— it's a sure sign of a lack of fit for the team.

It's Not a Sprint, It's a Marathon

Recruiting and hiring take a lot of time. There are no silver bullets that make it easy, speed it up, or guarantee a higher hit rate. It's work. Disregarding the process and guidelines shared in this chapter will lead it to feeling not only like a marathon, but one through mud, wearing ankle weights.

A candidate accepting an offer provides a brief respite from this toil. Celebrate, then get ready for them joining the team (onboarding is discussed in Chapter 8). But recognize that even with the opening filled, the process of recruiting is never finished. Keep working on other open reqs. If there are none, design leaders must still be prepared for the contingency of a member leaving their team. While sourcing and interviewing might not be happening at all times, networking and talent identification are ongoing activities, even if they move to the background when there are not specific roles to fill.

[7]

Developing the Team: Professional Growth and Managing People

In Chapter 3, we stated that one of the qualities of successful design organizations is that they "treat team members as people, not resources." This quality is most evident in how people are managed, and how their professional growth is supported. Companies may question why they should do so much for their staff—isn't a good job with a steady paycheck enough? Considering the difficulty of finding, hiring, and retaining talent in this heated design job market, investing time in thoughtful management and professional development pays dividends in three ways every business will appreciate:

Reputation

Quality improves as team members are more deeply engaged, bolstering the company's reputation as a place to do good design work.

Retention

Churn is reduced, lowering recruiting costs and the overhead of onboarding.

Recruiting

Team members become advocates for joining the team, saving additional recruiting expenses.

Levels Framework for Designers

Any design organization has a responsibility to grow their people. Given that design is a craft of practice, the primary means for such growth are widening and deepening design skills. In addition, as the designer becomes more senior, growth must also take into account soft skills and leadership skills, those that help them not just work with others but get the most out of them.

LEVELS AND CAREER PATHS

Many companies use a framework of levels to chart the seniority of employees. Typically, human resources (HR) teams use levels to calibrate employees across different functions, to make things easier in matters such as compensation. The risk of working with levels is adopting a bureaucratic stance, seeing team members not as people, but as resources within a certain band of experience. Do not let levels define the team. Instead, use levels from the perspective of the team members, who are eager to understand how they can grow and evolve in their careers. Done right, levels are the scaffolding that helps team members elevate.

Levels and career paths should be made explicit during the recruiting and hiring process. A consideration for many candidates is how they will be able to grow as professionals. A clear, designer-driven leveling structure with charted paths gives the candidate confidence that the company will be supportive in their development.

We propose five basic levels of growth for members of a design organization, whether those members remain individual contributors or become managers. These levels should not be taken as universal—they will need interpretation and modification to fit within a company's existing scheme.

Our leveling framework has a series of criteria to assess a team member's progress:

Theme

This is the overarching professional theme for the team member at this level, the orientation and focus for their development.

Title

A list of suggested titles for people working at this level.

Achievements

Concrete accomplishments in the member's career that have gotten them to this level. Typically companies use "*x* years' experience," but that should be of secondary concern to what they've actually done.

Scope

The scope and scale of the work this person is expected to do.

Process

Their relationship to a broader design and development process.

People

What is this person's relationship with people on their team, and with people on other teams?

Cross-functional meetings

Though this may seem a minor detail, what role this person plays in cross-functional meetings (i.e., with the product development team, or shareouts to executives) is a strong indicator of their influence and visiblity.

Core skills

How they deepen and add core design skills (outlined in the next section).

Soft skills

Working as a designer is just as much about working as designing. There are interpersonal skills that enable becoming a reliable and productive member of a team.

Leadership skills

As designers advance, it is important that they not only develop their design craft, but embrace leadership skills that will help their ideas and positions be realized.

The levels framework holds regardless of whether the team member has direct reports. We are avoiding the unfortunate practice of many companies to bind the idea of "career growth" with "becoming management," where the only way for someone to advance in their career is by managing other people. Engineering organizations have long known that leadership and management are not the same, and someone can drive the efforts of a team, even a bunch of teams, without being responsible for their team's day-to-day management. Design organizations should follow suit. Going through our five levels, a team member may be an individual or contributor. After presenting those levels, we dig into the Manager Path, and the qualities of a successful design manager.

CORE DESIGN SKILLS

A vast range of skills—more than any one person could be expected to master—are necessary to deliver great product and service design. Each skill is grounded in a deep discipline with its own processes and tools:

User research
> Conducting user research sessions (in-home, in-office, user testing, diary studies), and deriving meaningful insights through analysis.

Information architecture
> Structuring content, developing taxonomies, crafting navigation, and formulating other activities that make information accessible, usable, and understandable.

Interaction design
> The structural design of a software interface, supporting a user's flow through a system and ability to successfully interact.

Visual design
> Color, composition, typography, visual hierarchy, and brand expression that present the product or service in a way that not only is clear and approachable, but appropriately exhibits personality.

Writing
> Clear written communication that, like good design, guides the user through an experience. Much of the time, written content *is* the experience, and far more valuable than the design dress around it.

Service design
> Systems-level understanding of all the parts (technical systems, frontline employees, touchpoints, etc.) that go into delivering a service, coordinated to support customer journeys.

Prototyping
> Quickly simulating proposed designs in order to better judge their user experience. Could be technical (writing code) or a patchwork use of tools like After Effects, Keynote, Axure, and Invision.

Frontend development

Delivery of production-ready frontend code. Valuable in ensuring that designs are implemented as proposed.

Given this variety, how a team member grows their skills is variable, depending on the designer's desires, mindset, and inclination. What matters is that, in order to progress, designers must deepen existing skills and add new ones.

The Myth of the Design Unicorn

In Silicon Valley, there's fetishization of the "full-stack" or "unicorn" designer, typically someone delivering interaction design, visual design, and frontend development. This is unfortunate, as no designer can be truly great across these skills, and this emphasis on technical execution serves to minimize design's potential. The less technical skills are more strategic, and set design up for greater impact.

LEVEL 1: BECOMING A DESIGN PROFESSIONAL

THEME	DEVELOP THEIR CRAFT AND PROFESSIONALISM
Title	Junior Product Designer
	Junior Communications Designer
	Junior Content Strategist
	Junior UX Researcher
Achievements	Right out of school, roughly 0–2 years' experience; quality portfolio
Scope	Solve specific function-level problems (e.g., add item to shopping cart)
Process	Work within process established by team lead
People	Part of a team that they've been assigned to
Cross-functional meetings	Attending the meeting
Core skills	Strong in one, capable in two others
Soft skills	Professionalism
Leadership skills	Not applicable

We begin with people right out of school, or who have made a career switch into design. This is an entry-level role, and no professional experience is expected. That said, even at this early stage, people must have some portfolio of work, either from school, or personal projects taken on in order to demonstrate their capability and promise.

At this level, the point is to simply become a design professional, focusing on deepening and widening their skillset.

Core skills

Ideally, even at Level 1, the team member is strong at one of the core design skills, and capable in a couple others. One typical template is the graduate of a graphic or communication design program who is strong in visual design, and has shown capability in interaction design and prototyping. Another template is someone shifting from a writing background into digital product design, who is strong in writing, and capable in user research and information architecture.

Soft skills

The discussion of soft skills throughout these levels is meant to be additive—new ones are developed over time, and none are left behind. The first soft skill to acquire is *professionalism*. Show up on time. Listen. Contribute. Respect peers. For people who have worked for a while, this might seem overly basic, but it's worth recognizing these are skills that need to be learned, particularly by those just coming out of school, but sometimes even by those who should know better.

Responsibilities

As we discuss responsibilities level by level, we will use the example of working in a company delivering ecommerce. At this level, the focus of work is on the details of execution, typically for function-level challenges, such as "add item to shopping cart."

People are on teams created by someone else, work within a process established by someone else, and look to their team lead for direction. In cross-functional meetings, they are a mostly silent presence, contributing when asked about their particular area.

LEVEL 2: THE SOLID CONTRIBUTOR

THEME	DEEPEN THEIR CRAFT, TALK ABOUT THEIR WORK
Title	Designer Content Strategist UX Researcher
Achievements	Roughly 2–5 years' experience; contributed to a couple of shipped projects
Scope	Given specific product capabilities that need to be solved (e.g., shopping cart)
Process	Work within a process established by team lead
People	Part of a team they've been assigned to
Cross-functional meetings	Contributing to the meeting
Core skills	Strong in two, capable in two others
Soft skills	Communication and presentation
Leadership skills	Not applicable

This designer's portfolio now shows their contributions to a couple of shipped projects, featuring less school work.

As with the prior level, they are still primarily focused on deepening and widening their core skills. As they are now being given some influence and even authority, it becomes essential that they learn how to talk about their work, particularly explaining their design decisions, in a convincing manner.

Core skills

They can strongly execute in two design skills, and are capable in two others. The specific path is less important than is the demonstration of deepening and widening of skills. Table 7-1 shows how that progress might happen from Levels 1 to 3.

TABLE 7-1. Two possible skills paths for two different roles (items in **bold** are acquired or improved at that level)

	CAPABLE	STRONG	EXPERT
Product Designer			
Level 1	Interaction Design Prototyping	Visual Design	
Level 2	Prototyping **Frontend Development**	Visual Design **Interaction Design**	
Level 3	Frontend Development **User Research**	Visual Design **Prototyping**	Interaction Design
UX Researcher			
Level 1	Writing **Interaction Design**	User Research	
Level 2	Writing **Service Design**	User Research **Interaction Design**	
Level 3	Writing **Information Architecture**	Interaction Design **Service Design**	User Research

Soft skills

While continuing to deepen their professionalism from Level 1, the new soft skill most in need at Level 2 is *communication and presentation*. Designers often wish for the work to speak for itself, that the rightness of a solution is self-evident. The reality is that if designers want their work to be realized, they need to know how to talk about it, present it, and articulate a clear rationale for the decisions that led to it.

Responsibilities

Execution details are still the primary focus, though the scope has shifted from function-level specifics to broader feature-level responsibilities, so from "add item to shopping cart" to "shopping cart." They are still a member of a team created by someone else, work within a process established by someone else, and look to their team lead for direction. Given their broader purview, in cross-functional meetings, they are expected to provide greater contribution.

The designer also becomes a more integral member of the design organization, supporting recruiting and hiring practices, and contributing to the ongoing development of the team's culture.

LEVEL 3: STEPPING UP—FROM DOER TO LEADER

THEME	TRANSITION FROM DOER TO LEADER, UNDERSTANDING THE BUSINESS CONTEXT OF THEIR WORK
Title	Senior Designer
	Senior Content Strategist
	Senior UX Researcher
	Design Manager
Achievements	Roughly 5–10 years' experience; contributed to multiple shipped products
Scope	Lead the solution of a product area (e.g., "the conversion funnel")
Process	Develop the process/approach for tackling a problem
People	Leading a team that's been given to you; collaborating with cross-functional peers
Cross-functional meetings	Driving the meeting
Core skills	Expert in one, strong in two, capable in two others
Soft skills	Facilitation, listening
Leadership skills	Strategy, empathy, and compassion

To achieve Level 3, team members have a portfolio featuring multiple shipped products; it should no longer contain schoolwork. Arriving at this level, they have demonstrated their understanding of the broader context in which their designs live, the intersection of business, technical, and customer factors that allow their work to be successful. They might not know how to navigate these interests, but they recognize their importance.

This level requires the first big professional shift for the team member. To succeed means knowing when to set aside design and focus on the interpersonal aspects of work. No longer is it simply about practicing their craft. They acquire new leadership skills and develop a serious shift in mindset. They must appreciate how all the core design skills, not just those they directly practice, work together to produce a great experience. Understanding the business context in which they're operating becomes important in driving better design decisions. This shift may prove challenging for designers whose success up to this point has been all about how they practiced their craft.

Managers need to play an active role in helping team members navigate this shift. Engage in hands-on coaching, spending more one-on-one time in order to provide guidance through specific challenges. Suggest leadership and communication skills training that will give team members tools to better facilitate, present, and persuade.

It takes about five years for someone to get to Level 3. It then takes around five years to get through it. Team members must grow in their design practice, their people skills, and their leadership ability before moving on.

Core skills
People at Level 3 continue to deepen their skills, though perhaps not at the rapid pace of the prior two levels. Shown in Table 7-1, as they move through this level, they should develop expertise in at least one skill, strength in two others, and competency in two more.

Soft skills
As the team member tackles bigger, hairier challenges, their scope becomes too complex for any one person to solve completely on their own. Grappling with this complexity requires designers getting ideas out of others, and so designers must develop the soft skill of *facilitation*.

To develop empathy and to facilitate successfully requires the team member to not just hear what others have to say, but to develop their skill of *listening*. Learn to devote undivided attention and appreciate interpersonal nuances. Be open to opinions and perspectives that challenge existing beliefs, and be willing to evolve their stance based on new information.

Leadership skills

To succeed at Level 3, it is imperative to acquire leadership skills. The first is the ability to engage in *strategy*, no longer just executing the "how," but articulating the "what" and "why" for a product and service. To conduct strategy is to make clear the trade-offs and positioning within business, technical, and customer contexts.

Along with strategy, this is the time to develop *empathy and compassion*. People who are caught up in their own thoughts, and their own perspectives, will have trouble leading. Developing a sense of empathy helps people better understand their colleagues, and engage them from their perspectives. Demonstrations of compassion make clear that other's interests are being taken to heart.

Responsibilities

With growth, the scope of responsibilities further widens, from specific features to more holistic product areas. Continuing our ecommerce example, the shift would be from "shopping cart" to "the conversion funnel," the sequence that takes a shopper from a product description through to payment. Team members at this level continue to work on the execution of design, but importantly, begin to spend more time on product definition activities, collaborating with cross-functional peers on figuring out just what to make, and then coordinate the efforts of other design team members to deliver quality work. They are now responsible for developing the process and approach for solving the problem, and leading others toward that solution. In cross-functional meetings, they are not just contributing, but setting the agenda and driving the conversation.

Team members deepen their responsibilities to the team in such matters as recruiting, hiring, and developing culture. This includes handling phone screens, conducting Career Day visits at colleges, and being part of on-site interview panels.

LEVEL 4: TAKING CHARGE

THEME	ESTABLISH THE BUSINESS CONTEXT, DEVELOP STRATEGY
Title	Lead Designer
	Lead Content Strategist
	Lead UX Researcher
Achievements	Roughly 10–15 years' experience; delivered successful work at the scope of "product areas"
Scope	Leading the solution of undefined problem spaces (e.g., "How do people complete a transaction?")
Process	Develop the process/approach for tackling a problem
People	Creating the team you need; defining the problem with cross-functional leads
Cross-functional meetings	Driving the meeting
Core skills	Expert in one, strong in two, capable in two others
Soft skills	Confidence and swagger
Leadership skills	Planning, mentorship

This team member has led design through development and launch of several successful products and services. They have a proven track record of strategic thinking that shows they arrive at intelligent design decisions.

Level 4 requires confidence in coordinating with peers in business and technology to not just understand and implement against someone else's strategy, but to craft that strategy. These leaders oversee a set of concurrent workstreams, requiring not only broad creative leadership, but a comfort in establishing process and conducting planning.

Core skills

Unlike previous levels, mastery of core design skills is not the primary marker of professional growth. Yes, team members should continue their mastery, but the reality is that in order for them to excel, it's less about how well they practice their skills, and more about how they lead others through the delivery of great design work.

Soft skills

A shrinking violet will struggle leading multiple teams and coordinating with accomplished peers across functions. To succeed at this level requires developing the soft skill of projecting *confidence* and even exhibiting *swagger*. This isn't about cockiness or arrogance—that kind of overbearing display turns people away. But by demonstrating an abiding faith in the rightness of idea, offering a vision that compels people to follow, leaders encourage others to join them in making that idea a reality.

Leadership skills

Going from Level 3 to Level 4 is to move from "little L" to "big L" leadership. The organizational expectation is that they are rallying teams to deliver great work. Team members at this level may have multiple smaller teams they are overseeing, requiring coordination to ensure effectiveness. This requires skills around *planning*, figuring out how a team will realize a strategy. This also requires a rich understanding of a range of design tools and methods, the time and effort it takes to practice them, and how to coordinate and deploy them to achieve desired results.

Getting the most out of a team means expending effort developing the members of that team. If this hasn't happened organically already, it is at this level where *mentorship* becomes a necessary skill. Leaders gain leverage through coaching less experienced designers, improving their practices. They also garner respect from their team, both through the demonstration of their mastery, and in their willingness to spend time helping others.

Responsibilities

The scope again shifts beyond already-known point solutions and features, and toward shaping products and services at a more holistic level. Team members are no longer given known problems to solve ("the conversion funnel," common to all ecommerce), but instead have to start by framing a problem before tackling it ("How do people transact with our service?"). This reframing means this leader is no longer following "best practices," but is setting themselves up to invent new ways of thinking about a problem, which enables innovation.

To deliver on this promise, team members are actively leading product definition, including planning, strategy, and the prioritization of work. They develop and drive initiatives such as style guides, pattern libraries, tackling new platforms, or generating wholly new product and service experiences. This broader mandate may require overseeing multiple workstreams within a program.

Outside of their design work, team members are responsible for elevating the organization. They recognize the headcount needs to deliver on their programs, and address it through recruiting and hiring. They support the professional development of their team members, whether through formal training and dedicated mentorship, or less formal coaching and advice.

LEVEL 5: THE COMPLETE DESIGN LEADER

THEME	ARTICULATE A COMPELLING VISION; HELP RUN THE COMPANY
Title	Principal Designer
	Design Director
	Creative Director
	VP of Design
Achievements	Roughly 15–20 years' experience; has led teams in framing and solving hard problems, and has driven innovative efforts that uncovered new value with new kinds of experiences
Scope	Entire user experiences (e.g., "What is the end-to-end shopper experience?")
Process	Establish a philosophy/mindset for how the team approaches its work (e.g., the Double Diamond)
People	Establishing the organizational structure, defining roles, opening headcount
Cross-functional meetings	Stakeholder for whom the meeting exists
Core skills	Expert in one, strong in two, capable in two others
Soft skills	No new ones, but continued refinement of existing ones
Leadership skills	Vision

And here we have our fully realized design leader. They lead multiple teams, and have become a peer to the company's executives, working with them to set direction. There is little time for hands-on design work beyond whiteboard sketches, and instead their efforts focus on activities with leverage—establishing processes, recruiting and hiring and composing teams, articulating visions that rally not just the design organization, but the company as a whole. Ultimately, team members at this level are accountable for the subject matter addressed throughout this book.

While the job titles have simplified and seem to focus on design—Principal Designer, Design Director, Creative Director, VP of Design—it's important to note that team members from any background, whether it's content strategy, prototyping, UX research, design program management, or design, can achieve this level.

Core skills

By this point, core design skills may begin to wane, in favor of leadership and soft skills—and that's OK. Skills such as planning, vision, and mentorship provide the leverage needed to direct the organization.

Leadership skills

One more leadership skill is necessary to adopt at this level: *vision*. This is the ability to create a narrative and representation that makes strategy concrete, and provides a "north star" and inspiration for the teams building toward it. Driving this allows design leadership to stand out, from leadership of other functions. The leader's success in this skill is not just in the development of a vision—the corporate world is littered with concept videos, detailed mockups, and other scenarios of possible futures. Their success is instead shown in how the vision catalyzes action, inspiring the people within a company to charge forward because they want to live in a world where that vision is made a reality.

Responsibilities

Level 3 was about understanding strategy, Level 4 was about creating strategy and the planning to realize it, and Level 5 is about crafting and selling a vision that compels an organization to embrace that strategy. At this level, the team member's impact goes beyond their team and direct peers. Their purview is to frame the end-to-end user experience for their company's customers, and to establish the processes and mindsets to achieve it. Their efforts influence the work of large swaths of the organization, and prove crucial for setting the agenda for the company.

A fundamental shift occurs in their relationship to cross-functional meetings. Where before they planned and drove the meeting, now they are a stakeholder for whom the meeting exists. They contribute through feedback and review.

Team members at this level are the architects of the design organization, and the standard bearers of its culture. They run internal meetings, and get funding and make plans for events such as team offsites. It's important to develop relationships with operations people in order to support the design organization—working with people in facilities to make sure the design space supports collaborative and visual work or partnering with HR to rework standard professional development practices to better support the needs of designers. They join other executives in annual planning initiatives, forecasting headcount and budget needs to keep the team effective and engaged.

The Manager Path

Intentionally, the prior discussion of levels is meant to be agnostic of whether the team member has people directly reporting to them or not. We took care not to address matters of people management, only creative leadership.

That said, as a design organization grows, it needs managers. These are folks who are eager to take part in the professional development of their team members. They exhibit empathy and compassion, and are able to navigate the messiness of people, and the variety of emotions that come into play.

The Manager Path appears at Level 3. At this level, someone interested in people management may take on a direct report, most likely someone at Level 1 who is new to the team. As managers grow, they take on more people. By Level 5, they become a Design Director or VP of Design, and may have other managers they are now managing.

Managers continue to keep their hand in creative work, appropriate to their level on the team, though they cannot be expected to devote as much time to it, given their management responsibilities.

Their skills and professional development evolve pretty much the same as those of individual contributors, with one key difference—they dig much deeper into the soft skill of empathy and compassion. Managers are the engine that drives everything discussed in this chapter, and as such they will benefit from receiving training and coaching specific to people management.

RULES OF THUMB FOR MANAGING DESIGNERS

Managing designers is different than managing design. Design is a process that is best managed within team contexts, driven by creative leadership. What we're addressing here is managing designers, the people, where the focus should be on helping them as professionals.

As an employee class, designers were millennials before there were millennials, and much of what is being written in the business press about new management practices has long applied to them. The following rules of thumb might not feel revolutionary, but are necessary to keep in mind when working with designers.

Set clear expectations

Like other professionals, designers can be quite goal oriented, and are eager to succeed. Unlike other professionals, success can be challenging to define. Whereas a salesperson can have a clear goal of a certain dollar amount of sales in a quarter, designers' goals are harder to articulate, because their work is collaborative by nature, and so any one person's impact is less direct. Some companies have tried measuring designers' work in terms of the amount of output, but that makes as much sense as rewarding engineers for the number of lines of code—quantity is not quality. Work with team members to make clear what is expected from them. For more junior members, whose work is farthest from direct impact, set expectations around improving their craft and learning processes, and developing the people skills necessary in a professional context. As designers become more senior, shift expectations to delivery, impact, and organizational influence. Consider factors such as the scope of projects, how many workstreams they are driving, timeliness and quality of their work, and their ability to productively engage senior executives. Because each team member is on their own journey, it's important to manage expectations person by person, and resist the temptation to set middle-of-the-road standards everyone can meet. Tailoring growth plans to individuals encourages them to be the best they can be.

Support, don't manage

After setting expectations, the next step is to help team members achieve them. Avoid telling people how to do their work—this is the kind of behavior that gave the word "management" a negative association. While that may have been appropriate in companies geared toward mass work such as manufacturing or industry (and it's debatable whether it was there), it's never been the best way to engage people in creative or knowledge work. Instead, encourage the team member's autonomy, and help them develop their own plan to achieve those expectations. When given ownership of not just their work product but also how they arrive there, the team member is even more driven to deliver.

Help remove obstacles

Team members often find themselves blocked, unable to make progress, but unclear as to exactly why they can't move forward. Sometimes it's a hangup in the creative process, where the proposed design solutions just aren't feeling right, and the team is spinning its wheels. Leaders identify when the team is slowed, and figure out ways to regain traction. A story: Not long after iPad launched, Peter led a team creating a cross-device ecommerce experience. The solutions for web and mobile were great, but the work for tablet was uninspired. Peter basically called "time out" and encouraged the team to stop designing, and to instead go back a few steps and think hard about what it means to deliver an experience on this new device. After a 45-minute ideation session based on this new thinking, the team became unstuck and began again to produce great work.

Often, the solution isn't a matter of creative thinking, but interpersonal relationships. Team members may become frustrated working with others, particularly across functions, who don't understand their contribution, or a team lead might have trouble getting executives to appreciate a proposed solution. A common tactic designers take at these times is to try to design their way out of the problem, doubling down on the work. This proves ineffective, because the problem isn't the design, but how people communicate. The manager needs to help the team members engage in better conversations, reminding them to be sympathetic to others' perspectives, and coaching them on how to frame a more productive discussion.

Whatever the issue, it's important that the team member be encouraged to resolve the situation themselves; managers should only directly handle obstacles in matters requiring escalation.

Go to the mat when necessary

Management isn't just about support and enablement. Sometimes team members find themselves unfairly or inappropriately challenged, particularly by those more senior to them. In such situations, it can be easy for a manager to shrug and stay out of it, but that will confirm to team members that their best interests aren't at heart. Sometimes, managers need to risk their social capital with the broader organization in favor of standing up and fighting for their team.

Frequent feedback

Too often, managers wait until a formal performance review cycle to provide needed critical feedback. Successful managers are those who offer small feedback frequently, whether positive or negative. It's important that managers provide not only creative feedback. More important is feedback about being a professional and a member of the team, and what's working and what's not from this perspective. Creative feedback should handle itself through critique and review processes within the team. Professional feedback is the specific purview of the manager.

It's not about design

Designers and their managers can find themselves in a world where everything is about design. It's important that managers remind their teams that design is one function of many, and to illuminate the role design plays within the broader organization. The goal is not for the company to deliver great design, but to deliver a great product and service experience in a profitable manner.

Get to know them as people

Designers work best when they can bring their whole selves to their work, and not just behave as an employee. When managing designers, seek to understand who they are outside of work. Encourage presentations between team members about their passions, hobbies, and pastimes. Host lunches where people share food traditional to their cultural backgrounds. Take them out for after-work drinks. These activities deepen the bond between team members, and the trust and respect engendered will lead to better work.

THE PERSONAL PROFESSIONAL MISSION

There are many ways for people to grow, and a good design manager is sensitive to the particulars of each individual on their team. To better understand those particulars, we use a tool called the Personal Professional Mission. Ask each team member just what it is that motivates them. Why, in a universe of opportunities, did they make the choices that landed them in the role they have? It's a big idea that most people have never been asked about, and haven't considered deeply. It may require some time, and repeated conversations, to develop an answer. The Personal Professional Mission is key to understanding how the person will want to grow, and form the foundation of the relationship between a manager and an employee. This foundation will shape what is expected of that team member, and drive the charting of that employee's career path.

As an example of a Personal Professional Mission, Peter's is to make the world safe for great user experiences. This has pretty much been his animating principle since he first started blogging in 1998, and was perhaps most fully realized in the creation and development of Adaptive Path, a design consulting firm dedicated to advance the field of user experience. It also spurred his departure from Adaptive Path, because Peter felt that he could best tackle this mission from inside the enterprise. User experience no longer needed a laboratory for development, but instead required operationalizing in-house in order to deliver on the promise. It's also led to his writing this book that you are reading—enlightened organizational design provides remarkable leverage for supporting the delivery of better user experiences.

Design Community Participation and Leadership

Because design organizations are relatively small, team members may feel stymied in their growth within a company—there are only so many senior positions to go around. This requires cleverness in identifying other ways to support professional growth. One area many designers wish to pursue involves active participation in the broader design community, sharing ideas and case studies, and potentially being seen as a leader in the industry.

It used to be that only design agencies felt it worthwhile to support their team members' desires to speak and write about design, serving as a marketing vehicle that could drum up new business (as it worked for us at Adaptive Path). Designers working in-house typically found that the company discouraged such participation. There was no direct benefit, and it was seen as a distraction from doing the work. Also, companies feared that sensitive intellectual property may be shared. Now, however, given the Global War for Talent, public speaking and writing are seen as means to help recruiting, signaling to other designers that interesting work is taking place.

To support team members means more than just offering consent. To grow as an industry leader requires real commitment from the company. It means time taken away from hands-on design duties. It may require offering training for speaking and writing. If nothing else, a more senior member of the design organization will need to mentor the junior members on how to communicate effectively for public presentation. The team member will need help finding suitable speaking and writing opportunities, and will also probably need organizational cover to make sure their presentation or essay is approved by corporate communications. (We advocate a don't-ask-for-permission-but-beg-for-forgiveness approach, as corporate communications often loves the word "no".)

Investing in Professional Development

What are the means by which team members can develop? The most obvious are those that exist within the organization—guidance and mentorship. Given the nature of design craft, a team that encourages a guild-like atmosphere, with masters and apprentices, will go a long way to supporting development. Much of this mentorship will take place on the job and in the work, but time should also be set aside for more formal internal training in contexts such as lunch-and-learns and team offsites.

While great, this type of mentorship traffics in ideas the team is already familiar with. Budget should be set aside to promote exposure to new ideas. Bring in external speakers and teachers that can introduce new ways of working. Offer an education credit to each staff member, around US$2,000–3,000 per year, for conferences, books, evening classes, online courses. Try to not place too many restrictions on how the money is spent—make clear it's for growth, and demonstrate trust in the team members by letting them figure out how they can best use the funds.

Growth Through the Organization

The very nature of the organization itself supports a form of growth. For junior members of the team (Levels 1 and 2), find a cadence for circulating them from team to team within the design organization. This way they get exposed to a wider range of problems, ways of working, and types of leadership. They also are less susceptible to burning out. Don't overdo it—the value of the Centralized Partnership is the committed relationship that allows designers to really dig into a problem and understand it deeply. Rotating staff too frequently will bring an unwelcome disruption to flow and team character.

More senior designers necessarily settle into working with a particular part of the business, and should be discouraged from circulation. Their relationship with cross-functional leaders such as product managers and engineers is crucial for maintaining the perceived value of design. That said, shifts can happen on the order of years if a design lead feels like they've given a particular area all they have to offer.

An opportunity for growth that design leadership might have trouble accepting is for people to leave the design organization for other functions in the company, such as product management or marketing. While a Head of Design may hate losing a valued team member, it's never worth restraining someone. In fact, such cross-functional movement can prove a boon to the design organization, providing advocates and accomplices throughout the company.

Climbing the Corporate Trellis

Professional development is often described as "climbing the corporate ladder." It implies the employee has a careerist bent, and a narrow, steady focus to reach the next rung. Often, such a linear orientation is not of interest to designers. Many don't seek to climb so much as to grow. Their motivations are more internal, pursuing mastery, seeking autonomy, following threads of personal interest, and tackling challenges that align with passions. This bushy, meandering growth is more like climbing the corporate trellis.

The leaders of the organization serve as gardeners, nurturing this growth, encouraging this progress, recognizing that the acquisition of skills means team members move laterally before they continue heading up.

These leaders need to hold firm on their criteria for levels. Team members may chafe at their placement and seek accelerated growth. Remind them that these levels are not restraints to hold them down, but simply benchmarks of their progress. If someone is sped through, they will not develop sufficient depth of craft or skill, and will be given responsibilities where they cannot meet expectations. It is crucial to set team members up for success as they grow.

It is not all on the team's leadership. Designers are responsible for charting that path, and accepting the reality of what will allow them to succeed. If they want positions of organizational power and authority, they will need to use non-design skills, letting go of their craft in favor of more leveraged activities. This might mean sitting in more meetings, reading and sending more email, staring at more spreadsheets, and preparing more presentations, but it's through these activities that they will have greater impact. For people who went to design school and have their identity wrapped up in their practice, this shift may prove challenging, leading to a crisis of confidence. Their managers must help them through this transformation, making explicit the connections between non-design leadership activities and their goals.

[8]

Creating a Design Culture

CORPORATE CULTURE IS AN INCREASINGLY IMPORTANT SUBJECT WITHIN MANAGEMENT CIRCLES, as evidenced by its coverage in business magazines and websites ("Organizational Culture" is among the most popular topics at HBR.org), and how some companies are rebranding HR as "People and Culture." Much of this focus on culture stems from a reaction to millennials now being the largest generation in the workforce,[1] and the perception that millennials have a different approach to work than their predecessors, with greater expectation for connection and meaning in the workplace, and less of a focus on simply getting paid. Too often, culture is interpreted superficially, but it's no longer enough to offer free lunches, onsite laundry services, or foosball. Considering people spend 90,000 hours at work over the course of their careers,[2] it makes sense for them to seek employment that is fulfilling.

When design leaders address matters of corporate culture, it is typically from the perspective of shifting a company's culture in order to embrace design. Before that happens, we implore: *Design leader, heal thyself.* Design's inability to have meaningful organizational impact is often the result of an unintentional or polluted team culture. Before attempting broad, company-wide change, make sure the design team's culture has been purposefully constructed to encourage the best work.

The Elements of Culture

It's one thing to have a vision for a culture. It's another thing to deliver on it every day. To break down culture into actionable items, we use the simple framework illustrated in Figure 8-1.

---

1 Generation X was the dominant generation in the workforce for only three years, much to the chagrin of both authors.

2 Pryce-Jones, Jessica, *Happiness at Work,* (John Wiley & Sons, 2010).

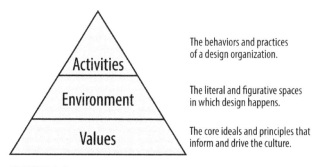

The behaviors and practices of a design organization.

The literal and figurative spaces in which design happens.

The core ideals and principles that inform and drive the culture.

FIGURE 8-1

A simple framework for understanding the components of design culture

It begins with *Values*, which form the bedrock of a team's culture. These are the mindset and principles the team upholds. Those values are made manifest through an *Environment*, the figurative and literal context and spaces in which the team works. And then the values and environment in turn drive *Activities*, the behaviors and practices of the team. In this chapter, we unpack each element to show how a design culture can get built.

Values

Values are the core ideals, principles, and tenets of an organization. Countries have them—USA: Life, Liberty, and the Pursuit of Happiness; France: *Liberté, Egalité, Fraternité*. Most modern companies articulate a set of values in order to communicate what they stand for. USAA, the financial and insurance services firm for American military members and their families, operates by the values of Service, Loyalty, Honesty, and Integrity. Facebook's 5 Core Values are Be Bold, Focus on Impact, Move Fast, Be Open, and Build Social Value. IBM opted for three statements: Dedication to every client's success; Innovation that matters—for our company and for the world; Trust and personal responsibility in all relationships. When written clearly and used appropriately, values attract talent that is appropriate for the company, and help the company make decisions.

Design organizations should make their values explicit as well. If the broader company has them, then they cascade down, though will need modification to be specifically meaningful. For example, Kristin works at Capital One in the design organization with a focus on helping customers use money wisely and designing for positive impact. As the design organization considers what to work on, it prioritizes time and effort on those initiatives that reflect the following values:

- Work from a shared understanding of human context

- Collaborate broadly and deeply, partnering better

- Coordinate efforts across projects, LOBs, and channels

- Prioritize the moments that maximize impact

- Measure the impact of our work, both human and business

THERE IS NO ONE BEST DESIGN CULTURE

While there are mindsets and practices that tend to support higher quality design, there is no one best design culture that all teams should strive to realize. Given the different values of different companies, and the variety of the services they deliver, it is up to each design team to articulate a culture that matters to them. While Peter was at Groupon, he established a culture in response to the marketplace Groupon was building, and the journeys that both merchants and shoppers were on. To deliver on these end-to-end service experiences, the design team's culture emphasized service design and collaboration. This in turn influenced hiring (bringing people on who were comfortable with user research, and worked well in teams), and delivery (encouraging more robust exploration of problems, deeper user research and analysis, greater coordination across designers). Other design teams may place greater value in building a "maker" culture (emphasizing prototyping, building, coding, and direct ownership of the design that is delivered) or one of strong aesthetics and personality (inclined toward storytellers and craftspeople).

And not only is it important to articulate values, but also a team's purpose (as was discussed in Chapter 3). Why does the design organization exist? How will it serve the rest of the organization? For example, when Bob Baxley led the design team at Pinterest, they were focused on predictably producing world-class work with quality and velocity. Kaaren Hanson, VP of Design at Medallia, an enterprise software company focused on managing customer experience, has stated the purpose is to craft exceptional experiences with empathy and thoughtful provocation. At Groupon, it was to ensure delight and coherence across the ecommerce marketplace.

THAT SAID...

While there is no One Best Design Culture, there is a set of values that are common among strong design teams:

Collaboration and support
> Our challenges are too big for any one person to take on. Collaboration is key to success, and when team members are challenged, designers pitch in for one another.

Respect for maker time
> While collaboration is essential, it's not the only thing. As craftspeople, designers need blocks of "maker time," being able to work without distraction.

Give and take critique with grace
> To get to the best quality output, team members must feel comfortable providing candid critique, without fear that it will hurt another's feelings and damage relationships. People giving the critique must do so respectfully.[3]

Inclusivity
> Great ideas and input can come from anyone, regardless of experience, title, or background. Strong teams encourage this broad engagement, making sure that every voice is heard.

Establish and uphold quality
> Every design team is measured by the quality of their work, and it's the responsibility of those teams to define quality.

It's about the work, not the ego
> Designers put a lot of themselves in their work, and can become wrapped up in the quality of their ideas. A strong design culture recognizes this personal investment, but also acknowledges that the work, the result, is what is paramount, not any individual's ego.

Having clear values and purposes that individuals and teams align to means that everyone understands when a team takes a customer-first approach, supports collaboration, protects making time, and seeks

---

3　For a compelling overview of how to create an environment of meaningful guidance, check out Kim Scott's *Radical Candor* (St. Martin's, 2017).

measurement for their outcomes. With that understanding in place, design leadership can advocate for and prioritize initiatives and activities like spinning up a customer insights team and repository, bringing customers and potential customers into concepting exercises, journey mapping training, and the development of common metrics. These objectives can then be tied back to performance management. Armed with the values, decisions both large and small are more easily made.

ARTICULATE YOUR CHARTER

Just like with the Magna Carta, the Declaration of Independence, or the Universal Declaration of Human Rights, an organization's values, principles, and purpose ought to be written down. In Chapter 3, we suggested the start of a charter for a broadly impactful design team:

> We're not here just to make it pretty or easy to use. Through empathy, we ensure meaning and utility. With craft, we elicit understanding and desire. We wrangle the complexity of our offering to deliver a clear, coherent, and satisfying experience from start to finish.

Once the purpose has been stated, add the team's values and objectives. Try to make it concise enough to fit on a single page, something that can be posted in a common area. Make it part of the conversation when recruiting and hiring, and refer to it in meetings and work sessions.

The act of drafting a charter is a remarkable exercise for a team to go through. It will be contentious, and force people to deeply consider just why they're doing what they're doing. The result, a printed document, is the first step to making the abstract and potentially nebulous notion of "values" into something concrete. The next step is shaping the space that upholds these values to support the work.

Environment

"We shape our buildings, and afterwards our buildings shape us."
WINSTON CHURCHILL

The environments in which work happens have a direct impact on the nature and quality of the work produced. It's crucial that these spaces, physical and virtual, manifest the values of the design organization. In turn, those spaces will enable new kinds of work previously unconsidered.

PHYSICAL ENVIRONMENTS

We saw the importance of environments come to life at Adaptive Path. When the company began, we worked out of our homes, and then for a few years rented a couple of rooms as a space where we could meet and talk. Our work focused on web user experiences, largely executing on interaction design and information architecture challenges for marketing organizations. In 2005, the company moved to a new dedicated office, a place we committed to being in every day, with large open spaces to support our work. And with this move, the nature of our work changed. Previously, work sessions involved going into a conference room, collaborating, and then having to take the material down when the meeting was done. Now, dedicated project spaces allowed us to keep our work on walls at all times (Figures 8-2 and 8-3). This externalization of a team's work product made it easier to share, to get feedback from others, and to introduce to our clients. The bigness of the space supported the bigness of our ideas, and our work evolved from execution-focused web user experience to strategic and definition-oriented service design and future forecasting. The big spaces in turn supported the work becoming more physical and tactile, with large diagrams, walls of concept designs, and Post-it notes everywhere. By freeing ourselves from working only within screen-based digital tools, we found ourselves tackling new challenges.

FIGURE 8-2
Project team at Adaptive Path, with movable walls behind them (the white wall is whiteboard, and the blue wall is a tackable surface). Photo by Peter Merholz.

FIGURE 8-3
The same workspace as shown in Figure 8-2, from the opposite angle—plenty of wallspace supports permanent placement of guiding documents such as experience principles. Photo by Peter Merholz.

It is for these reasons that so many design firms operate in such an open, studio environment. And space management has become one of the more quotidian challenges as design organizations are built in-house. It is still common for offices to be divvied up into cubicles, with fluorescent-lit conference rooms with one whiteboard as the only places where people can come together to collaborate; design teams are often spread out across floors, buildings, and campuses. These environments are death to creativity and innovation.

Firms that embrace design seriously invest in creating physical environments that support healthy cultures. At MX 2015, Katie Dill, director of Experience Design for Airbnb, shared her team's mantra of "Know the moments that matter. Keep it simple. Make it visual. Ensure it's visible." They partnered with Gensler to create an award-winning studio space that supports collaboration with no shortage of wall space to showcase work and remind the team and visitors that they're in the business of creating a sense of belonging in the world. Their physical space is directly connected to their purpose (Figure 8-4).

FIGURE 8-4

The Airbnb design team at work. Blackboards for posting work, floor-to-ceiling whiteboards, a table stocked with creative supplies, and even some art on the wall. One the left, you see the edge of a large HD display. These elements invite collaboration. Image courtesy of Airbnb.

Pinterest has enormous flat screen TVs throughout their space showcasing the latest explorations from the design team. And when Catherine Courage joined DocuSign as their SVP of Customer Experience, she met with Facilities in her first week to ensure that dedicated space for design was prioritized.[4] This can take the shape of dedicated collaboration spaces like project rooms, video-enabled conference rooms, and workshop/training spaces, as well as space in high-traffic areas to show work in progress, upcoming releases, and design explorations.

When Kaaren Hanson joined Medallia as VP of Design, she created physical space and invited partners to rotate teams through. She organized the visits into two-week sessions with daily themes not only for the work but for meals and activities. She treated the sessions as immersive learning opportunities and even created customized menus for each of the partner team members, taking into account any dietary preferences. She leveraged her team's culture to prioritize building relationships with key partners, celebrating the diversity of skills and perspectives, and quickly had a long list of other teams asking to partake in upcoming sessions.

STUFF ON SHELVES AND WALLS

A common practice in design firms that has not widely taken root as design moves in-house is the creation of a library. These libraries feature two types of books:

- Informative tomes discussing methods, case studies, design history, and the like

- Sources of inspiration, such as design annuals, studio monographs, and other primarily pictorial collections

Even in this Internet-connected age, not all the best information can be found online (we say, writing a book), and an assortment of smartly curated books can serve as a means of connecting and uplifting a team (Figure 8-5).

---

4   Ms. Courage and Ms. Hanson shared these stories when we spoke with them for this book.

FIGURE 8-5

Adaptive Path's library. Books constantly flow in and out, and there's even a card catalog to keep it all in order! Photo by Kristin Skinner.

Shelves are not the only spaces to be curated. The walls of the design area should also serve as a display for exemplars of art and design that can serve as inspirations to the team.

Shelves and walls aren't just for material made outside the company. Every project should be printed, archived, and cataloged for reference, and key artifacts that demonstrate the team's quality standards should be showcased on walls or countertops. Such displays reinforce the commitment to quality, communicating to the team, partners, and visitors the standards that deserve to be upheld.

WHERE DO PEOPLE SIT?

When the product development team is small, it's easy for designers, engineers, and product managers to all sit together. As the team scales within the building and across geographies, it becomes necessary to explicitly decide where team members sit—do they sit with other designers, even if they're not working on the same problems, or do they sit with their respective teams, co-locating with engineers, product management, or marketing?

Ideally, the answer can be "both." A healthy approach is for designers to spend chunks of time in both contexts, where execution time is spent with the cross-functional team, and reflection and review time happens among other designers. This requires both a design studio space and available desk space within cross-functional teams. If space is at a premium and a choice must be made, then it's a matter of "it depends." If the design team is relatively new, or in a period of low morale, they makes sense to keep the designers together to bolster their culture and sense of belonging. As the design team matures, it become less reliant on constant contact, at which point it makes sense to shift designer focus to their respective teams. This also has the effect of spreading the design mindset to other parts of the organization.

VIRTUAL ENVIRONMENTS

While it's great to have the whole team sitting together, it's not always feasible or appropriate. It's important to manage an organization's virtual environments as purposefully as their physical ones, and to imbue them with the team's values.

What we're about to say feels self-evident, but warrants saying as we have been in multiple environments that tried to operate this way: email is not a collaborative work tool. Too often companies still resort to email as the way to handle communications, make and track decisions, and share ideas (as attachments). It's messy, as oftentimes not all the appropriate participants are included (and have to be awkwardly added into email threads after they've begun), and the record of decision making is hard to parse as separate threads emerge. Even worse, many large enterprises automatically delete email every 30 to 45 days or so, wreaking havoc on one's ability to refresh on important topics.

For a design team to work in a virtual environment, it's important to do so with tools suited for collaboration: chat tools like Slack or HipChat; project communication and coordination tools like Basecamp, Asana, and Trello; shared file servers like Box and Dropbox; cloud-based collaborative productivity tools like Google Apps and Mural.ly, and design feedback tools like Wake.

Simply having tools is not sufficient. Standards and practices must be articulated and enforced to ensure that they are used in a way conducive to teamwork. As anyone who has spent too long finding the right funny animated GIF for a chat conversation can tell you, these collaborative tools can become a distraction and attention drain when not handled appropriately. Shared file servers only work if people can find what they're looking for. Communication services only work if people don't neglect them and resort to email.

Based on our experience working on and leading design teams across locations and time zones, we've come up with a set of considerations to maximize team time, protect maker time, and allow for spontaneous collaboration:

- For *quick conversations*, use chat.

- For *discussions*, use video conferencing versus phone as your de facto communication tool. This ensures that you're able to experience and interpret non-verbal cues like body language, expressions, and the like. This is crucial in staying connected while on distributed teams.

- When *video conferencing isn't feasible*—often meetings happen on the way to another location, the connection speeds sucks, you're at the airport, etc.—it's important that your colleagues are comfortable getting and making phone calls. There's no doubt that more will get done and that everyone involved will feel better about it.

- *Collaborate* over Google Docs/Sheets/Drawings or something similar. There is little brainstorming that can't be done virtually using Drawings to replicate a sticky note exercise; Sheets to track and analyze data like estimates, budgets, forecasting, and prioritization; and Docs for communication, feedback, and capturing decisions.

- *Install cameras* to show the walls and all the collaboration in each location.

- Decide as a team where and how you will *distribute and version your files*. Use Dropbox for design team collaboration; Basecamp for communication and fileshare for files "for review" or "final"; and if dealing with customer data, Box to ensure regulatory compliance.

Activities

The design team typically doesn't have total control over their environment—they have to share space with other teams, the Facilities department restricts what can be altered, and there might simply not be budget to make significant changes. What the design team *does* have total control over are the activities that constitute their day-to-day work. How people behave is the most meaningful embodiment of a team's values. Most of that behavior will be rooted in basic friendliness and professionalism, but it's worth stepping back and applying intentionality to how a team acts, both internally and with people in other functions.

ONBOARDING

A special class of activities takes place when a new member joins the team. Thoughtful onboarding is the difference between a new member feeling welcome, knowing where stuff is, and hitting the ground running, or someone feeling confused, uncertain, and unable to work. Provide the new designer with a team roster, instructions on the shared file structure, pointers to standards and guidelines, a glossary of acronyms and other jargon, and a buddy to go to for questions as they arise. Make sure they have a computer with everything they need already installed (which might mean working with IT to get a "designer special" setup, as designers have needs for software, displays, and accessories that differ from other departments). Schedule a team lunch to celebrate the new member.

At Groupon, the design organization called itself the Design Union, a recognition of the company's Chicago roots, and a celebration of the honest labor and craft of the team's design work. Every new team member received a welcome kit, which included a branded notebook (Figure 8-6) and a rubber stamp featuring the Design Union's shield (Figure 8-7). These small, fun non-essentials made clear the importance of craft within the team.

FIGURE 8-6
Branded notebook for Groupon's Design Union

FIGURE 8-7
The Design Union's
rubber stamp

MEETINGS

Just seeing the word "meeting" elicits groans. The problem, though, isn't meetings. It's poorly run meetings with no clear agenda, no one keeping matters on topic and on time, and loud voices dominating the conversation. When effective, meetings serve a crucial role for a design team and its culture, primarily around communicating effectively, but also solidifying the team's identity through shared work.

A weekly meeting for the design organization should have these three elements:

News and information from the rest of the company

These days, most company news is presented in email or all-hands meetings. Within the design organization meeting, leadership can provide further context for this news and information, highlighting what's specifically pertinent to the design team. Leadership then solicits feedback to be shared with other company leadership.

News and information about the design organization

As the design organization grows, team members no longer "just know" everything that's going on within the team. The weekly meeting serves as a formal means to share such updates. Of particular interest will be any open headcount, and how recruiting and hiring is going for those positions. This also serves as an appropriate time for team members to share high points (successful launches, positive external feedback) and challenges (blockers to doing great work, issues with tools and processes). Be careful that these meetings don't turn into pity parties—it's easy for the sharing of challenges to devolve into unproductive griping and

moaning. If genuine concerns are raised that are worth addressing, note them, make it clear that they will be addressed outside
the meeting, and share updates at subsequent meetings.

Show work, discuss a topic, share inspiration

A design team meeting without some engagement in the work
feels lifeless and bureaucratic. The nature of what is shared can
change week by week. Once the information-sharing aspects of
the meeting are handled, make sure there's enough time for the
team to get into something addressing the craft of design. It could
be showing work (either completed or in progress) that helps other
team members appreciate exactly what is happening across the
team. Or someone might choose to present on a topic, such as a
new method, or the clever use of a new tool. Or perhaps someone
just shares something (a video, a book, a product or service experience) that inspires them in their work.

Regardless of how large the team gets, keep these meetings to no more
than one hour per week.

DOING THE WORK

All of this effort to create the right environment and explicit mindset is
for naught if your team isn't able to deliver. In Chapter 3, we described
the difficulty of striking the balance between establishing a quality bar
with valuing delivery over perfection. However that balance is struck,
what's crucial is that the team is able to produce. Companies inadvertently throw a lot of obstacles (unnecessary meetings, unreasonable
deadlines, unclear requirements) in the way of design work, and the
most important mark of the team's culture is how it navigates these
obstacles and successfully delivers.

Meetings are perhaps the force most disruptive to a design team's ability to produce. This is less of an issue in small organizations; as companies get bigger, meetings seemingly grow exponentially. Designers
find their calendars carved up with colored squares, leaving very little time to do their design work. Successful design work requires the
ability to focus for long stretches, ideally in a space with other design
team members. One way to address this is to protect designers' time
in a predictable way—no meetings before noon, or no meetings on
Tuesdays and Thursdays. This can be tough to stick to, because at some
of those meetings, important things are discussed that would benefit

from designer involvement. To make sure design's perspective is represented, a team lead or other design leader should be tapped to attend such meetings, keep their team's time free, and make sure that they remain up to date.

As a team scales, it can prove helpful to establish a predictable cadence of design work. When Bob Baxley was leading product design at Pinterest, he developed a schedule of "closed-loop" theme weeks.[5] Mondays are called "Playground" with a focus on generating ideas. Tuesdays are "Collaborate," where ideas generated or iterated on Mondays are shared and discussed with partners from product management and engineering. Wednesday's focus is "Breathe," providing room and space for teams and individuals to go deeper on ideas and topics. Thursdays are reserved for "Workshops" to evaluate with teams, and Fridays are "Product Reviews" with an executive audience. Establishing such a clear, repeatable rhythm for the work allows other teams to adapt their meeting times accordingly.

Along with a dependable work cadence, another factor that helps teams as they scale are design guidelines. Based on core brand attributes and desired experience principles, these guidelines help teams not have to invent their designs from scratch, but instead provide a framework that supports the speedier development of new material while retaining quality. Some companies, like IBM, make these available publicly for other teams to leverage as a baseline or for inspiration. At GE, they couldn't hire enough designers to cover all the work that needed to get done, so they built a UI framework for everyone to use. Their goal in building and extending a design system was to help teams that couldn't get UX designers be successful. They took a risk by spending time to do something no one was asking them to do, but in the end they gave design the chance to have a greater impact.

PROVIDING CRITIQUE

A key mechanism for design to maintain its quality standards are review sessions, often called critiques. During a critique, designers present their work to one another, and receive feedback for how to make the work better. Because folks are putting their work out there

---

5   This information comes from our interview with Bob Baxley.

for others to criticize, it can be a stressful experience. A strong design culture is one where people eagerly seek out this commentary; a symptom of a troubled culture is one where such review practices leave people deflated, or even in tears.

Being mindful of a few principles can make critique a positive experience for the team, and serve its purpose of maintaining a high quality bar:

Designers should provide multiple solutions

When sharing designs to be reviewed, designers often share a single solution to a particular problem. Inevitably, this is a solution they've put a lot of effort into, and if the feedback is critical, the designer may walk away defeated. Instead, designers should present multiple solutions to a problem (there is always more than one way to solve a design problem). This provides healthy distance between the designer and their suggested solutions, enabling them to critique their own work by discussing trade-offs. It allows the discussion to be one of shared problem solving, as opposed to defending one particular direction.

Orient feedback in terms of objectives and results, not preference

Critique doesn't happen in a vacuum. There is a lot of context that leads to a suggested solution. If that context isn't shared as part of the critique, then the feedback devolves to matters of preference ("I don't like that shade of green," "That design is cluttered"). When presenting work, make sure the stage is set by sharing the desired objectives and results of the designs. This allows team members to phrase their feedback in terms that drive toward helping solve the problem ("Those multiple calls to action will distract people from the primary conversion path," "The visual style is quite cool and corporate, not the homespun and artisanal aesthetic the brand stands for").

Be respectful, but candid

Given that these sessions happen among colleagues, it's crucial that they show respect for one another. Avoid derogatory or demeaning language ("this sucks," "what a mess," "how could you have thought this was a good idea?"), as it will only put the recipient in a defensive stance, closing them off to any legitimate critique provided. That said, a critique has to be a space where it's OK to be direct, even if the commentary is not "nice." Politeness and niceness are fine for social gatherings among strangers, but will be the death of design quality. No one is being done any favors if they are told their work is "fine" when in fact it isn't measuring up to the team's standards. Any designer worth their salt welcomes constructive critical feedback.

Everyone gets a turn to comment, and leaders comment last (if at all)

Make space for everyone in the room to provide feedback. Critique must be a place where the quality of the commentary, not the seniority of the commenter, is most important. That said, people will react differently to what leaders say. If a leader makes a comment early in the session, it may shut down further discussion, as folks might assume the matter settled. For that reason, leaders should comment last, only after everyone else has given their input. At that time, the leaders might find they don't need to say anything, as their commentary was already provided by someone else.

There is a lot more that can be said about productive critique than we can get to here. *Discussing Design* (O'Reilly, 2015), by Adam Connor and Aaron Irizarry, is an excellent book for digging deep into this topic.

EXPOSURE TO CUSTOMERS

A key sign of a healthy design culture is how often designers engage directly with customers. Whether shadowing sales calls, listening in on customer support, or going out in the field and observing use, by exposing themselves to the everyday contexts their users are facing, designers adopt not only empathy, but humility, reinforcing their role in serving others.

CROSS-TEAM COLLABORATION

One of the most effective ways to spread culture within a design organization is to find ways to mix up the people working in it, so that team members get exposed to colleagues beyond those on their immediate team. The challenge is doing this in a way that is not too disruptive, as team constancy is necessary when digging in and delivering good work.

A simple approach for this that we developed at Adaptive Path is the Open Design Session. In an Open Design Session, one design team shares out a particularly sticky problem they're tackling to the rest of the design organization, who roll up their sleeves and pitch ideas for how to tackle it. For the host design team, the benefit is they get fresh thinking on a problem they've stared at for too long, and often receive insights that allow them to move forward. For the other designers, they get to step away from their normal work for a little bit, and apply themselves to a new problem. They also get to see what their colleagues are doing elsewhere in the organization, and broaden their overall understanding of the service they're working to deliver. And everyone benefits from working side by side and seeing how others think through design challenges.

Open Design Sessions typically last for about an hour—it's rarely feasible to ask more of others' time. To get the most out of that hour, the host team must come prepared, with a clear framing of the problem in question, the design objectives, and any research or other input material. The setup should take about 10 minutes, and then the designers work, typically sketching ideas, for 30–40 minutes. The remaining time is for sharing out the designs.

In order for Open Design Sessions to be a habit, it helps to keep them regularly scheduled. At Adaptive Path, we had two each week, with different orientations. The first was on Tuesday mornings, and was meant to be "generative"—coming up with new ideas and solutions for the problem being posed. The second was Thursday afternoons, and these were meant to be more evaluative—productive critique of the work a team did. These afternoon ones also included beer, which helped keep the sessions lighter and friendlier.

DESIGN COMMUNITY INVOLVEMENT

Activities important to embodying a design culture don't occur only within the organization. For any design team that has a core value around the engagement, development, and promotion of ideas, a key way to demonstrate that value is with the design community at large. Start with small efforts, like lunch-and-learns, inviting people from outside the company to speak to the team. Connect with the local community through associations such as the IxDA, AIGA, UXPA, and the like, and offer to host evening events. Encourage team members to share their ideas, methods, and case studies at conferences or through writing. Supporting these efforts means allowing team members the time to engage. If it truly is a cultural value, it shouldn't be that difficult to make work.

Spreading Culture

With a robust, effective working culture in place, the design organization now has the foundation upon which to bring design centricity to the rest of the company. Making the charter explicit helps others know how to get the most out of working with design, and what to expect from that process.

While the design team's environment exists primarily to support how they work, a key secondary benefit worth planning for is how it allows people from other disciplines to better connect with design. Of most obvious import are the collaborative workspaces, whether physical or virtual, where design hosts cross-functional conversations. By creating spaces where anyone feels welcome to contribute, design becomes appreciated for its ability not just to execute, but to spur the right conversations that drive progress.

Then there are the by-products of investing in such environments. Welcoming spaces, with comfy chairs, books on shelves, and appealing art on the walls, will be magnets for people throughout the company seeking a convivial place to work. When the efforts of the design team are made external and explicit (posted on walls and on large displays), visitors see all the work that design is doing, and initiate serendipitous conversations that go beyond the immediate tasks at hand.

In the next chapter, we dig into how design can best work across functions. Establishing a strong culture empowers designers to operate from a position of confidence when engaging with their peers.

[9]

Successful Interaction
with Other Disciplines

"If you want to go fast, go alone. If you want to go far, go together."
AFRICAN PROVERB

In Chapter 2, we asserted that design can play a role in each stage of development from idea to final offering, and that it should be woven into every aspect of the service from marketing to product to customer support. The challenge is that most organizations are structured and run in a way that keeps design as a phase in a production chain, as opposed to an activity that permeates the business. Designers are typically hired or added to a team too far downstream in a product or service lifecycle, and funding models don't take into account the need to hire designers who aren't specifically aligned to a product or service. In fact, most enterprise funding models are structured to support individual lines of business, further siloing designers and discouraging cross-lines of business collaboration. In the past, designers subsumed their work to cater to how other disciplines operated. In order to be most effective, design must collaborate with other disciplines and needs to maintain its own identity and practice.

Cross-functional teams have become ubiquitous because companies must accelerate speed to market; it's essential that leaders pay attention to the way these teams are set up and how well they work. Yet, in a 2015 *Harvard Business Review* article, Behnam Tabrizi shared that of 95 teams in 25 leading corporations, nearly 75% of cross-functional teams are dysfunctional.[1] They fail on at least three of five criteria:

---

1 *https://hbr.org/2015/06/75-of-cross-functional-teams-are-dysfunctional*

- Meeting a planned budget

- Staying on schedule

- Adhering to specifications

- Meeting customer expectations

- Maintaining alignment with the company's corporate goals

The main reason why most cross-functional teams fail is because silos tend to perpetuate themselves. However, projects that had strong governance support—either by a higher-level cross-functional team or by a single high-level executive champion—had a 76% success rate.

For design to succeed cross-functionally, it must have clear leadership and be seen as a peer. This means both organizationally—directors of design working with directors of product management, engineering— but also in terms of the specific people doing the design work. While the field of design has a deep history, its broad involvement within enterprises is recent. Because it's not a mature internal discipline, its practitioners are generally less mature, which can make engaging with product management and engineering as a true peer exponentially challenging. Often outnumbered within cross-functional teams where there's an acute focus on shorter iterations, it can be difficult for a lone designer to advocate for seemingly minute details, like animated transitions, that impact the experience. Great design is difficult to achieve in a reductive process or environment that is keenly focused on speed and efficiency.

So how can collaboration with other disciplines be approached in a way that is achievable, sustainable, and impactful?

The initial step has been the subject of this book up to this point— solidifying and elevating the design organization to ready it for making significant impact. Now it's time to leverage all of the foundation, output, and management qualities in place to focus on successfully interacting with other disciplines. Plenty has been written about "how product teams should work," usually with an orientation around a mindset and methodology such as Agile or Lean. We believe that every project should have an end-to-end accountable leader; clearly established goals, resources, and deadlines; and built-in review cycles to measure progress and plan for adjustments. That said, we are purposefully not delving into processes and methods (Scrum, standups, backlogs, sprint planning, burndowns, file management, specifications, etc.), as addressing them in detail warrants its own book. For our purposes, we focus on principles and practices that support strong cross-functional work, from the perspective of the design organization. Examples include:

- Reinforcing the goal of defining and delivering a great experience from the customer perspective

- Ensuring that design recognizes its role on the cross-functional team and demonstrates humility and equality

- Developing, adapting, or following an agreed-upon design process best suited to objectives and the product/service

- Acknowledging openly and often that organizational structure is perhaps the number one challenge for cross-functional teams and making an explicit goal to embrace this constraint

Phase 1: Achievable

Don Norman, widely known for his books on design, particularly *The Design of Everyday Things* (Basic Books), and his advocacy for user-centered design, has said "Complex things can be made understandable; that is the role of good design" and that "Managing this complexity and producing the things to tame complexity takes partnership." At this stage, it's crucial that design leaders work with business and technology leaders to wrangle organizational complexity by making agreements about business and experience goals and priorities, roadmaps, and funding, and identify and clear any potential roadblocks before the cross-functional team can get to work. This process of influence, negotiation, and definition is essential at the outset of any cross-team initiative in order to determine that the work to be done will be achievable.

The Definition phase of the Double Diamond framework addresses the steps needed to articulate a strategy and develop a plan for the offering. Perhaps most importantly, this phase relies on cross-discipline collaboration in that everyone (or, at least, product management, design, and engineering) is in the mix together, tightly collaborating to define the vision for the product/service. Because this cross-discipline work can feel quite messy, particularly when team members have not worked together before, make time to establish the team's working relationships, paying particular attention to the four areas we'll now discuss.

CLEAR DECISION MAKING

Leadership of the group can be a significant challenge with cross-functional teams, and in large organizations, a governance model may be required. At the outset, and any time the focus of the work shifts, ensure that there is someone responsible for making decisions and articulating the rationale. At Adaptive Path, we utilize stakeholder maps (Figure 9-1) at the outset of an initiative as a scoping and planning tool to define core, direct, and indirect stakeholders as well as understand business needs/value and customer needs/value.

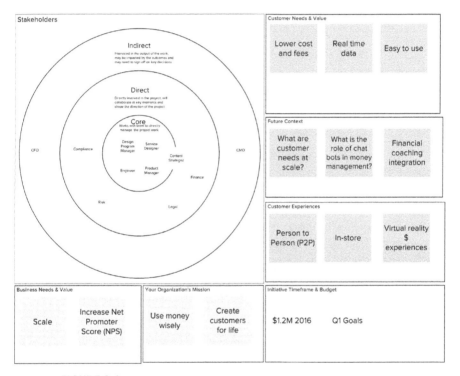

FIGURE 9-1

Stakeholder map and scoping poster used to collaborate and guide planning discussions. Perhaps most important for the design team to define and articulate are: Customer Needs & Value and the Customer Experiences that this initiative will create or improve.

We've found this simple tool effective in driving the conversation and decision about who will ultimately be responsible for approvals. It's also useful in identifying gaps in knowledge or alignment. If significant gaps are identified, that signals that the program isn't ready for kickoff.

DESIGN TEAM AS GATING FUNCTION

We have worked at companies that tried to do too much with the teams they had. As a result, designers were spread thin, projects were half-baked, and once something was launched, it was then neglected. We've also seen improbable ratios of 20 product managers to 1 designer assigned with a never-ending backlog. Instead, focus on what's achievable by examining the design team's skills alongside the constraints of time and budget to focus on what's achievable. Design's role in the planning process should have three key elements:

- Bring an empathetic perspective that understands what customers will find desirable

- Use design methods such as sketching and prototyping to make the requirements concrete

- Focus and scope the work

In order to focus, the design organization must have mechanisms in place for saying "yes," "no," or "not yet" to the work itself. Kristin spoke with a design leader who, when she first joined her new company, had a team of 14 designers. In her first few weeks, she observed that a single designer was assigned to support, on average, 5–7 "technology pods," each led by a product manager and a development lead, and composed of developers and testers. At the same time, the frequency and variety of additional requests for design support overwhelmed the number of designers on the team.

She soon hired two design program managers to focus on intake (qualification, prioritization, pipeline) and capacity planning. Over the course of eight weeks or so, they met with each business leader to better understand their roadmaps and top one or two priorities. They then led full-day, deep-dive sessions to understand the problem space, human and business objectives, and stage(s) of work. With this data in hand, they could assess skill sets needed and align design talents to formulate a design portfolio plan.

The plan, easily captured in an Excel file to enable collaboration and revision history, included top-level initiatives, value to the customer, value to the business, a team-based approach and clearly defined team structure, skills needed, timeframe, and a hiring plan. By modeling human-centered design practices to better understand and scope the work with partners, they were able to articulate and support the #1 and #2 priority within each business group, enable and improve the partnership between design and product management to frame problems to focus on both the business and human value, align the right design skill sets paired with the right project(s) at the right time, and provide transparency across the business of the highest priorities for which design was aligned. This effort, while substantial, took about four months but allowed them to see connections and make better informed decisions. And in taking the time to understand the problem space and phase of each initiative, they were able to cover more with the same team.

MAINTAINING QUALITY

While quality is everyone's responsibility, it is the designer's responsibility to articulate, demonstrate, and uphold what quality means for the experience. This can run counter to the behaviors and processes that non-design team members—accustomed to being valued for delivering with speed and efficiency in their roles—bring that can discourage the quality of the experience.

Quality can be broadly interpreted to mean a standard of something as measured against something similar. In the design organization, it's easier to define and assess quality against other designs. But when in a cross-team setting, each team will bring their own definition and standards for quality. Take the time to ensure that everyone on the team understands what is meant by quality.

Ideally at the outset of the project, define what quality means by giving everyone on the team something to reference. This simplistic approach is especially important for teams working toward common goals, but from different disciplines. In our experience, we've addressed quality in several ways. We collected examples of high-quality design on our Basecamp site. The working space included an area for examples. And we included quality assessment as a lever for moving work from in-progress to ready for production.

DEFINED ROLES AND EXPECTATIONS

Clear goals, aligned leadership, focus, skill sets, and quality standards are essential for successful cross-team collaboration, but perhaps most important is the definition of roles and expectations for participation. Once the team has been identified, spend some time getting to know one another. Margaret Gould Stewart, now VP of Design at Facebook, created a set of attribute cards to use for setting expectations for individuals on teams. At Adaptive Path, we often used these sets to guide a "what we want from you" exercise to help set expectations about roles.

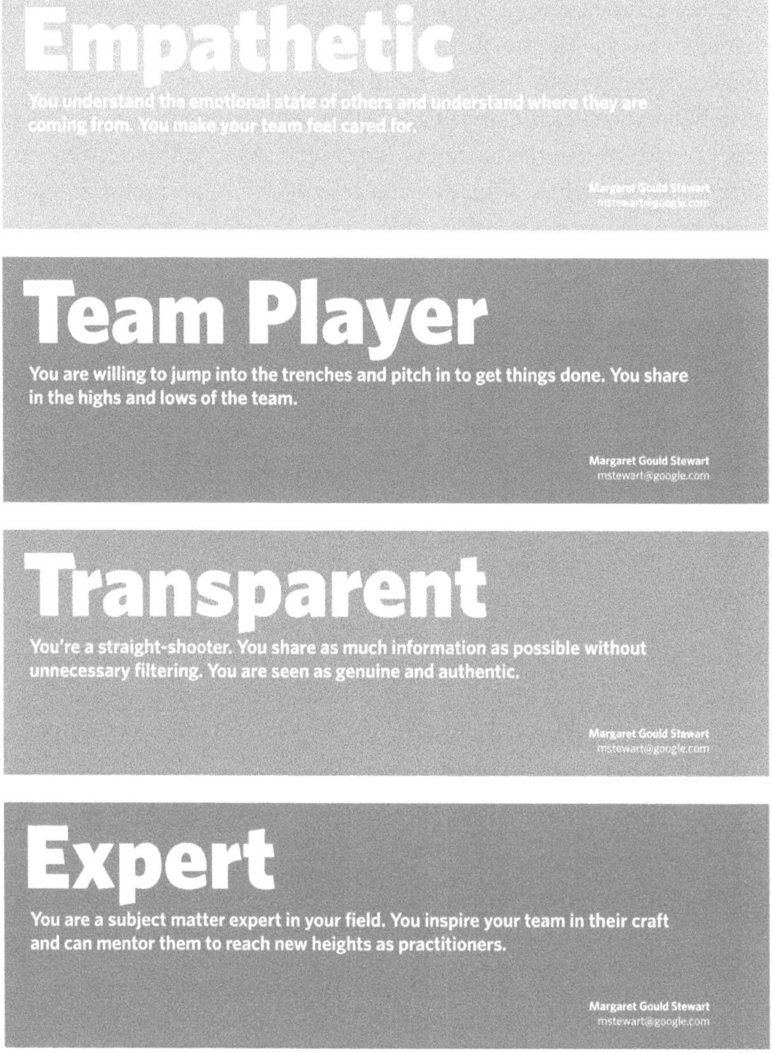

Empathetic
You understand the emotional state of others and understand where they are coming from. You make your team feel cared for.

Margaret Gould Stewart
mstewart@google.com

Team Player
You are willing to jump into the trenches and pitch in to get things done. You share in the highs and lows of the team.

Margaret Gould Stewart
mstewart@google.com

Transparent
You're a straight-shooter. You share as much information as possible without unnecessary filtering. You are seen as genuine and authentic.

Margaret Gould Stewart
mstewart@google.com

Expert
You are a subject matter expert in your field. You inspire your team in their craft and can mentor them to reach new heights as practitioners.

Margaret Gould Stewart
mstewart@google.com

FIGURE 9-2

A subset of printable attribute cards created by Margaret Gould Stewart and used by teams at Adaptive Path to help set expectations for team members

In the set there are 15 cards (Figure 9-2), each with an attribute and a description. At the outset of a project, the team would discuss and select the top 1 or 2 attributes we expected from each team member. We'd capture images of each team member holding their selected cards and post them somewhere prominent in the project space or via our project management site (Figure 9-3). Ideally, this exercise sparks conversation that flows to interests, strengths, and opportunities for growth and better collaboration. This can be especially useful on teams where people may not have yet worked together, and come at the problem from very different perspectives. Whatever the activity, it's important that teams have the opportunity to meet one another as people, rather than just showing up to play a role.

FIGURE 9-3
The cards in use—teammates choose 3–4 cards that describe the traits they most need from you, and photograph you holding up those cards

With clear goals, decision making, and roles and expectations defined, a clearer plan will evolve for the cross-functional team. It's during this stage that folks have a better sense of marching orders, and more typical design and engineering processes come into play.

Phase 2: Sustainable

In our conversations with Bob Baxley, he highlighted the importance of taking the time to "design the machine that designs the designs."[2] While the plan assumes that everything must fall into place in order to deliver, not explicitly stating how the work will be coordinated and facilitated across multiple workstreams and initiatives can prove disastrous. And simply inserting experience design methods into a development process will not improve the experience. To support the plan, it's essential that designers and the design team have clear direction and guidelines to protect maker time, communicate effectively, understand when and how to escalate issues, and gain insight into one another's work so that they can best map design tasks to the overarching schedule and roadmap.

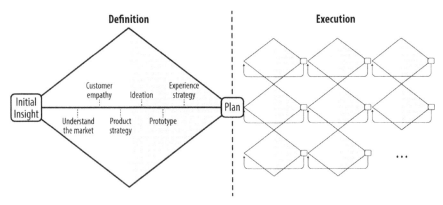

FIGURE 9-4
The team has shifted to the Execution phase of the Double Diamond model

PROTECTING MAKER TIME

In discussing design team culture, we mentioned the importance of protecting maker time within the design team. When a designer is working on a cross-functional team, the frequency and volume of meetings can increase exponentially, as the designer is inevitably juggling being part of both the design team and the cross-functional team. This can lead to zero time for actually doing the design work. As a team, take

---

2 Bob Baxley's talk on "Designing the machine that designs the designs" can be found here: *https://vimeo.com/166885565.*

the time to decide how to structure each week. Refer to the cadence we discussed in Chapter 8 or look to other teams who may already have a good solution. Identify blocks of protected time for doing the work and blocks of time for reviewing the work. For meetings that affect the team's work, but don't require designers to share out or collect feedback, send the design leads who can make decisions on behalf of the team and bring back information. Most importantly, ensure that the rest of the cross-functional team understands and respects the cadence of "making" versus "meeting" time, and that there is someone on point paying attention to and resolving any tensions that may arise.

Design leaders must remember to have frequent conversations about drawing boundaries, taking time to recharge, and setting a strong example of what proper work hours look like. Teams and individuals need to know that it's acceptable and encouraged to have a balanced work life.

OPERATING AGREEMENTS

Consider using an operating agreement to outline how to interact with one another and think about problems, and productively escalate issues for resolution.

Example of topics to include in an operating agreement:

- How we'll integrate as one team
- Communication plan
- Availability of key staff for work sessions
- How we'll work with the Insights group—access to key insights, and for new research, timing, recruiting, protocols, and field research
- Stakeholder approvals and timing
- Process for escalation and issue resolution
- Assumptions for deliverables—timing, type, and fidelity

To create an operating agreement, facilitate two sessions with the full team. In the first session, brainstorm ideas without judgment or discussion, then discuss ideas and build an affinity diagram. Let ideas rest for at least a day, then reconvene to review the work, discuss and modify any ideas or categories, and finalize the list. Finally, publish the operating agreement alongside or within your team charter as a one-pager or slide in a deck.

COMMUNICATION

Key to successful collaboration and healthy team dynamics is keeping everyone in the loop. Even if the updates are brief, daily or semi-daily communications through a project management tool like Basecamp go a long way to provide insights and confidence to other team members and stakeholders spread out across the organization.

Ensure that everyone on the team can speak each other's language. In large organizations, jargon can take on a life of its own, so encourage everyone to clarify terms. Create a document to capture terminology and frame discussions around goals and objectives.

When a design organization grows beyond 40 designers or so and is spread across different geographies, the challenge of staying connected grows exponentially. To address this, be explicit about expectations around insights and knowledge sharing. Designate a team to create and manage a shared insights repository for customer research. Create or carve out a role dedicated to "communications" or "storytelling" with responsibility for things like consistency of voice and tone, internal blog posts, guides and checklists for facilitating cross-team shareouts, newsletters, and internal event planning and coordination.

Phase 3: Impactful

Taking the time to establish a solid foundation focusing on achievability and sustainability will enable the team to be up and running, gaining velocity through growth and learning, and, ideally, delivering on the roadmap. At this stage, it's not just a matter of following a specific plan. Instead, continuous monitoring and adjustment to the plan is essential. It's also crucial that someone is assessing and addressing overall project health—team satisfaction, partner satisfaction, risks, success—on an ongoing basis, not just the progress toward milestones.

A design leader should reinforce that successful cross-functional teams think in terms of programs, not just projects. It's natural for participants on a team to focus on just their work streams and deadlines. The product lead and technology lead will present progress against business or performance metrics, and it's the design leader's responsibility to consistently frame discussions, meetings, and feedback through the experience lens. This means participating in customer research and bringing in research findings from customer interviews and call center transcripts to reflect back the experience that customers and potential customers are having.

At this stage, there should be a clear understanding of the design organization's maturity and the value that it provides. Roles and gaps have been clearly identified and a clearer path to get there will be evident. To ensure that cross-team collaboration is as impactful as it can be, we recommend these activities to monitor the team's impact:

Survey the team

> Ask everyone on the team two simple questions: What's working well? What's not working? Identify the top three in each category, as well as the overlaps, and put a plan in place to address them. Assign owners and small teams to lead initiatives. This should happen at regular intervals and any time a major milestone is completed.

Make a plan

> Analyze the survey data and map the results to business and customer value and use examples from other organizations both inside and outside the company. Call out any previous efforts and their results as to what worked and what didn't. Create actionable 30-, 60-, or 90-day plans for each initiative that outlines activities, outcomes, and support needed. This can be a one-sheet containing three columns for the timeframes and three rows for the activities, outcomes, and support.

Conclusion

Working cross-functionally should feel a little different than working within design. Remember to:

- Respect others' opinions and listen to everyone's points of view

- Challenge assumptions, but don't challenge individuals

- Articulate a rationale for design decisions

- Build the plan to account for high-friction milestones like handoffs between teams and on- and off-boarding team members

- Don't take things personally, but also don't tolerate negativity— address it directly

We believe that great teams design, build, and deliver great products and services. No one person, team, or organization should hold responsibility for the outcome. We also recognize that there will be innumerable challenges in getting to the ideal state when interacting with other disciplines and that none of the things we have outlined will be achievable without strong leadership and considerable peer influence. Consider our approach a north star, taking into account the conditions for success and challenges that exist, and adjust as needed to effect the desired outcome.

A Note on Cross-Functional Teams

For our purposes, we're considering cross-functional teams to mean a group dedicated to a particular problem space, initiative, or products. For digital product work, these teams are typically made up of a core team of designer, product manager, and engineer; for marketing and communication, the team may just be a marketing director and a communication designer. At different stages, and depending on the focus, the team could also have QA, release engineers, localization, and technical writers.

[10]

Parting Thoughts

IN MID-2016, AS WE put the finishing touches on this book, the field of design finds itself at an inflection point. The spread of software has driven the spread of design, but as companies embrace design, they realize it contains so much more potential than just making software easier to use. The challenge for designers is to embrace this window of opportunity, and to establish themselves as core to business.

We know that the models and frameworks proposed in this book are not achievable overnight. They are meant to serve as milestones, north stars, and guidelines for those embarking on the journey of making their design teams as effective as they can be. Because every organization is different, so are the paths they'll need to take.

Managing such change will be difficult, and will often not feel worth it. It is easier to maintain the status quo, even if that means design doesn't realize its potential. But don't give up! If old-guard companies like IBM (IBM! "Big Blue!"), SAP, and GE invest in design and invite it into the C-suite, then it's hard to understand why this couldn't happen anywhere. There is greater promise for design now than at any time in its history, and dedicated leaders are needed to turn that promise into reality.

The Untapped Opportunity for Design

Key to this promise is a curious and underappreciated by-product of the "designer/developer ratio" discussed in Chapter 6, a tool used to ensure an appropriate balance between these roles. In companies that seriously invest in design, that ratio is around 1:5 to 1:10. This means that the work of 40 designers, who could fit inside a large conference room, requires 200–400 engineers, who would need a movie theater to hold them; 40 is literally a manageable number—that many people can be successfully engaged in a facilitated conversation or workshop, where every voice is heard. That's not true of 400, or even 200—that number of people is simply too big to directly manage.

A brief story Peter was told: when a San Francisco fast-growth tech company moved to new headquarters, their team of 40 designers was placed in one room, a large studio space. An unintended consequence of this placement is that the CEO could go to this single room, look around at the work posted on walls and emanating from people's screens, and see what was happening across his entire company. The lens of design activity enables a perspective that no other function provides.

This story inspired Peter when he was at Groupon. The team was distributed, so no one room could serve this function. So, once a month, he gathered work from across the entire design team, and shared it out to product, marketing, engineering, and executive leadership. In roughly a single hour, he could present the entire breadth of Groupon's activity as seen through the lens of his team. After the first session, the CEO told him that it was already the most important meeting at the company. This is because nowhere else could you see such a broad scope in such a manageable fashion.

What these stories point out is that design can be a function with great leverage, where a relatively small number of people can have an outsized impact. However, most design teams are not ready to take advantage. This gets at the crux of why we've written this book—in order for design to capitalize on this remarkable opportunity, it needs to get its organizational act together. Creativity and talent are insufficient. Business savvy, strong leadership, and operational effectiveness must be brought to bear as well.

Designers need to throw off their self-imposed mental shackles of being a service function to other parts of the company. With confidence, evidence, and commitment, design teams will realize they have as much influence and authority as anyone. Maybe even more, as they are situated throughout the development lifecycle—research to uncover customer needs and desires, strategy and definition to articulate what should be built, and execution to turn those ideas into concrete offerings.

Keep Design Weird

As design increasingly moves in-house, designers find themselves in environments unintentionally hostile to good design practice. A measure of a design team, and its leadership, is how they navigate this.

Many design teams find themselves at one of two poles. We've seen a number of teams, whose leadership comes from design agencies, try to protect design by insulating themselves from the rest of the organization. Essentially, these teams try to re-create the studio model when moving in-house, but in doing so inhibit connection with the rest of the company. This may lead to great design work in the abstract, but it also ultimately leads to ineffectiveness, as without those connections, the work of the design team is not realized through the product or service.

The other pole is one of total integration. Product design molds itself to existing product development processes, usually some flavor of Agile. "The Business" drives key decision making around goals, objectives, and requirements, and the designers do their work within constraints established by others. This integration improves design's day-to-day effectiveness, but leads to subpar work. Design is a different kind of activity than engineering, and what works for technical development is not ideal for great design. By behaving as "team players," design becomes overly accommodating, and loses what makes it interesting in the first place.

And what makes design interesting is that, within corporate and enterprise contexts, it is weird. It can be soft, empathetic, touchy-feely, and expressive. People that have grown accustomed to hard, reductive, and dispassionate modes of operating may find such approaches disconcerting and off-putting. Instead of trying to conform in order to fit in, designers must respectfully maintain their distinct vantage. In Chapter 3, we discussed the importance of diverse perspectives when tackling problems, and what's true for design specifically is even truer for the organization as a whole.

The challenge for in-house teams is to figure out how to maintain that valuable creative spark while working in a way that still supports delivery.

Beyond Features and into a World of Experience

There exists a pattern in the evolution of technical product categories. Consider the Internet-connected smartphone. Among the first was the Nokia 9000 Communicator, released in 1996. It was ugly, underpowered, and difficult to use, but it proves historic as an early mobile device that connected to the Internet. This is the *technology* phase in evolution, where the mere ability to do something new is what is interesting.

As technology improved, there erupted a myriad of smartphones, from companies including Palm, BlackBerry, Microsoft, and Nokia. The devices competed on capabilities, such as handwriting support, cameras, speed of connectivity, battery life, and integration with other technologies and operating systems. This is the *features* phase, typically where marketing takes over, requiring more and more stuff added to the product so that more bullet points and checkmarks can be included on the box and in product reviews. The assumption is that the most feature-rich product is the best. However, these products are so bloated with capabilities that they are difficult to use, and people take advantage of only a small percentage of the features.

And then, in 2007, Apple entered the smartphone market with the iPhone. From a features standpoint, the iPhone did not measure up—it had barely a day of battery life, the EDGE network was slower than 3G, and there was no physical keyboard or stylus. Where iPhone excelled, though, was its thoughtfulness, integration, and ease of use, all in a handsome package.

This is the *experience* phase, where success is due not to how many capabilities are crammed into a product, but from the gestalt derived as a whole. Another recent example is collaborative chat software. When Slack launched, it had far fewer features than its powerful and more established rivals, but succeeded because it was far more straightforward to set up and use, and exhibited a delightful personality.

In Chapter 4, we introduced the Centralized Partnership, and depicted how a design team interfaces with product management and engineering (Figure 10-1).

Centralized Partnership

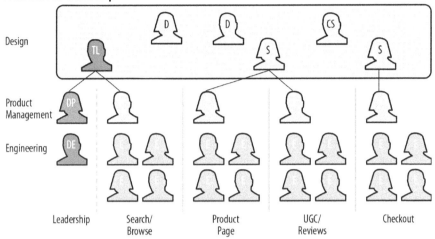

Design

Product
Management

Engineering

Leadership   Search/   Product   UGC/   Checkout
    Browse   Page   Reviews

FIGURE 10-1

How a Centralized Partnership design team works across product and
engineering teams

And while we firmly believe the Centralized Partnership is superior to
either full centralization, or embedded and decentralized design, this
diagram depicts a key drawback. The Centralized Partnership still conforms to the "features" world. Product teams have been constructed to
support ideal *engineering* team sizes (around 5–8 engineers), and there-
fore, have narrow purviews.

This diagram shows a team of six designers. That is the same number
of designers Peter and Kristin led on an ecommerce project for Adaptive
Path (his last project for the company). That team was not constrained
by an existing set of features. Instead, drawing on user research, the
team was encouraged to reconsider the entire online shopping *experience*. And that team of six designers not only delivered on Search
and Browse, Product Page, Reviews, and Checkout, but also Gifting,
Sharing, Wishlists, Merchandising, Social, Video Messaging, In-Store
Pickup, and a comprehensive style guide as well. When approaching
problems from an experience point of view, designers tackle not only
the obvious tentpole features, but all the smaller, more nuanced elements that turn something from being a collection of functions into a
coordinated whole.

This approach proves radical because it's not optimized for engineering delivery (and, as anyone working in technical product development knows, everything is optimized for engineering productivity). But because the experience mindset proves transformative in the value being delivered, with greater success realized when moving beyond the constraints of features, then supporting an ideal *design* team size must be seriously considered. The challenge is figuring out how to operationalize this so that the design work coordinates with engineering. We (the authors) don't have a specific answer for this. So we leave it as a provocation to the reader, look forward to hearing how others have made this work, and will include those successes in a second edition!

Index

About the Authors

Peter Merholz is an independent product and design executive. Prior to that, he co-founded Adaptive Path, the premiere user experience consultancy, helping lead it to international renown. He has maintained his personal site, *http://peterme.com*, for nearly 20 years, and coined the word "blog."

Kristin Skinner is Managing Director at Adaptive Path and Head of Design Management at Capital One, where she established and leads its Design Management practice. For over 16 years, she has led designers and design teams to deliver new product and service experiences, and speaks and teaches workshops on Design Management.

Colophon

The animal on the cover of *Org Design for Design Orgs* is a crimsontip longfin fish or coral devil (*Plesiops coeruleolineatus*). As its name suggests, the longfin fish has a long body that grows to between 8.5 and 10 centimeters. While its coloration varies, its body is usually black or brown with two dark stripes behind the eye. Its dorsal spines have orange or red tips with a bottom border of white, and the basal part of the dorsal fin has a blue stripe.

The crimsontip longfin can be found from the Red Sea and East Africa to the Samoa Islands, Oceania, and southern Japan. It can also be found as far south as Australia at Queensland. This species is described as "secretive" and lives in the shallow parts of outer reefs. It comes out at night, when it feeds on fish, gastropods, and small crustaceans.

Many of the animals on O'Reilly covers are endangered; all of them are important to the world. To learn more about how you can help, go to *http://animals.oreilly.com*.

The cover image is from *Lydekker's Royal Natural History*. The cover fonts are URW Typewriter and Guardian Sans. The text font is Adobe Minion Pro; the heading font is Adobe Myriad Condensed; and the code font is Dalton Maag's Ubuntu Mono.

Milton Keynes UK
Ingram Content Group UK Ltd.
UKHW021935171024
449785UK00008B/65